WE STILL HOLD THESE TRUTHS

AN AMERICAN MANIFESTO

Preserving the Heart of American Democracy in the 21st Century

Ronald L. Hirsch

"We Still Hold These Truths," by Ronald L. Hirsch. ISBN 1-58939-587-5.

Published 2004, 2005, 2011, 2018, 2025 by Virtualbookworm.com Publishing Inc., P.O. Box 9949, College Station, TX 77845, US. ©2004, 2005, 2011, 2018, 2025 Ronald L. Hirsch. All rights re-served. No part of this publication may be reproduced, stored in a retrieval system, or transmitted in any form or by any means, electronic, mechanical, recording or otherwise, without the prior written permission of Ronald L. Hirsch.

"*We Still Hold These Truths* is a concise, provocative, and challenging interpretation of the expectations, rights and obligations of citizens envisaged by the Founders in the Declaration of Independence and the Constitution.   A good, thought-provoking read for all who care about the pivotal issues facing the leaders of the United States."

—Michael Phillips,
VP (retired) Motorola International Inc.

"Integrating the founding principles of Democracy with an understanding of today's issues, *We Still Hold These Truths* is an expressive, call-to-action analysis of the need for mainstream Americans and traditional liberals to unite under a common philosophy   It is a timely work, addressing key topics that face Americans today. It is also a work of hope, and a call to return to a liberal perspective that seems lost in the special interest-dominated policies and agendas of the past 20 years."

—Marlan Buddingh,
Communications Director, In the Image

"As the nation approaches the 2004 election, the insightful comments, fresh approach, and fervor of Mr. Hirsch will provide a much-needed stimulus to policymakers, thought leaders, and the Democratic Party. It will also provide millions of moderate and liberal Americans who have been wandering in the desert of the Bush administration with a vision for our country and a call to action to which they will heartily respond."

—Elaine Weiss, former Regional Director
U.S. Dept. of Health and Human Services

To my parents, Max and Charly Hirsch, who valued freedom
and understood its concomitant responsibilities,
taught me concern for the well-being of others, and
imparted to me the principles of honesty and
personal responsibility.

TABLE OF CONTENTS

FOREWORD
to the 2025 Edition

20 years ago, I wrote this book because I felt that America and the Democratic Party had lost their way and that it was critical for the future of our democracy and republic to focus on what made America, America. What is it about this 250+ year experiment that made America, even with all of its problems, its shortcomings, special among nations?

Unfortunately, Party leaders paid no attention to what I said and so as time progressed, as one election followed another, the state of our nation and the welfare of its people deteriorated. This despite an energized economy and a phenomenal growth of wealth among the top 5% of U.S. citizens.

In the midst of this wealth, no one paid attention to the deterioration of life for the average worker, and so as their financial status worsened and the Democratic Party, which had been their home and their support, did little but mouth platitudes in their support, they turned with anger from the Party into the arms of Donald Trump. Not just once, but three times.

How did this political dysfunction come to pass? Election night, 2008 ... as Barack Obama walked to the podium to accept the presidency, I thought the urgent need for the message of *We Still Hold These Truths* had passed. The public had responded to Obama's message of hope and change and to a platform that incorporated many of the ideas presented in this book.

But that support was predicated on change, and when real change didn't happen after two terms, except for Obamacare, workers felt betrayed. So instead of hope, a specter of even greater darkness has fallen on this country's political landscape and its future.

What right-wing pundits started in 2008, Donald Trump honed to perfection in the 2016 campaign: the use of demagoguery and the big lie. With these tools, Trump and the pundits roused people who were angry and fearful to a fever pitch.

The same tactic was used in the '20 and '24 campaigns, each one bringing even more people into his fold with his promise of a better economy and living standard and casting illegal immigrants and the Democratic Party as scapegoats for the middle-class workers' problems.

That the lies became more outlandish and his meanness more evident made no difference. He, like other autocrats and dictators before him, had successfully created a towering persona that could do no wrong in the eyes of his followers. As he had the temerity to say in the 2016 campaign, he could shoot someone in the middle of 5th Avenue and he wouldn't lose any voters.

But why were, are, so many people so angry and fearful? Why were and are they open to this demagoguery? President Carter posited that their fear is of a changed social order evidenced by the election of a black president. While few stood with Carter on this, the depth of anger and fear and the way it has been aroused argue for racism being a factor.

When Sarah Palin talked about taking back *our* country and *real* Americans, who was she talking about? White, non-elite, conservative Christians. When Trump repeatedly railed against undocumented Hispanics using fear-inducing derogatory labels; when he lashed out against Muslims indiscriminately as a threat to this country (this was in 2016, not 2024); when he failed to condemn neo-Nazis – he sparked the nascent racism that lies within many people.

But racism is usually a scapegoat. What is provoking the underlying fear? The answer is, as Carter said, a changed social order.

The first aspect of that change is a reversal in the well-being of America's middle class. The middle class is made up mostly of nonprofessionals ... people with only a high school degree. As manufacturing and other middle class jobs have disappeared in both urban and rural areas over the past four decades, their standard of living and quality of life has been drifting downward. Even in the 2018 "full employment" economy, wages for workers with a high school education remained stagnant at a lower level than they were in the early 1970s. Not much has improved since.

Not only have reduced earnings resulted in economic problems for these men and their families, these pressures have brought about greater interpersonal stress, with a resulting increase in divorce rates and depression.[1] Reduced financial security has also resulted in increased antagonism toward those ... people of color and immigrants ... who are seen as a threat to their security.

Adding to their fear and anger is the letdown they felt, after 8 years of Obama, of nothing really changing in their lives, except for Obamacare, as I noted above. Dashed expectations are dangerous.

The second aspect of the changed social order is the prospect of white America becoming a minority. To be white used to confer on the white middle class a certain sense of status, but now they feel robbed of that status. Aggravating those feelings, they saw Democrats promoting programs to help people of color and the poor (perceived as primarily people of color), as well as other disadvantaged groups such as transsexuals and LGBT, while they saw their problems as getting no attention over the years. They felt forgotten; ignored.

Due to this changed social order, the world as the middle class knew it since WWII has been turned upside down. And this is not just an urban problem; it is rural as well. Small wonder they are scared, angry, and alienated.

Yet this important shift in the American social fabric was not really discussed by Democratic politicians during the 2016 or more recent campaigns, let alone during the past few decades. Yes, they talked about the need to protect the middle class, but the evisceration that had already occurred, the imbalance of Democratic Party policies, and the threat they felt from people of color was not addressed. That was left to Trump and his fellow Republicans, who brazenly exploited the situation.

The result is that we now have a country and parties divided ideologically as never before - both sides have become radicalized - with a substantial realignment that has hurt Democrats. For many, reasoning has disappeared from the process. If someone spouts the right party line, that's all they need to hear.

And so we now have Republicans controlling the White House, Congress, and 22 state governments. Further, Trump is even more

---

[1] Don Peck, "Can the Middle Class Be Saved," *The Atlantic*, September 2011

aggressive in his attempt to undermine most Federal agencies by installing heads and aides who are dedicated to disrupting the very mission of the agencies to protect the public. These men and women have been vetted primarily for their loyalty to him, not for competence.

The meanness of Trump and Republican legislators, their disregard of the public good, is shocking. Republicans, both in Congress and in state legislatures across the country, are trying to destroy much of the progressive framework that our national and state governments enacted over the course of the 20th century. During that time, government was transformed from one that protected business interests almost exclusively to one that recognized the need to stand behind those in our society who had no voice and no power ... the middle class, the working class, and the poor ... while still encouraging vigorous business activity.

Whether it's Obamacare, the Environmental Protection Agency, the right of workers to organize, progressive taxation, various programs that benefit the poor, or consumer protection, even education, Republicans seek to use their majorities to cut everything they detest from the role of government and leave people to fend for themselves.

Well, not quite all people. Despite all their previous talk of the need to cut deficits, Republican support for subsidizing business and the rich remains undiminished.

The issue is not simply big versus small government, high versus low taxes. The radical Republican Trumpist movement is attacking the heart of our democracy, our historic values. The radical Right seeks to fundamentally alter the balance that our nation has historically struck between private rights, the public good, and government.

In previous editions of this book, I said that, "If this charge sounds over the top to the reader." After the 2024 campaign, I think most readers will realize that this is not over the top. But let me quote from a commencement address given back in June 2005 by the always level-headed Bill Moyers. "A profound transformation is occurring in America as the balance between wealth and commonwealth is threatened. ... A broad range of the American commons is undergoing a powerful shift away from public responsibility and obligation to private control and exploitation. ... The basic constitutional principles of America are under assault."[2] The threat is even greater now.

What should the Democrats do in this alarming situation? How do the Democrats regain their majorities in Congress, retake the presidency, and save our country?

We need stronger campaigns that speak to a broad cross-section of the American public. Just listen to what Vice-President Mondale said just days after the 2004 election, "We really need to work on the question of what we are for. Unless we have a vision and the arguments to match, I don't think we're going to truly connect with the American people."

How sad and beyond belief that after a long and intense campaign, the quadrennial defining moment for the Party, it did not know the essence of what it stands for, what its vision is. How then could the American public?

That was the biggest problem I saw when I wrote this book in 2004: the lack of a vision, and not knowing how to speak to the people in a way that the people get. As a result, Democrats were not able to get people on the margins of life and others who needed to be convinced to cast their vote, to vote; probably more importantly, they didn't convince traditional Democratic-voting workers who were leaning to the other side to continue to vote Democratic. That's the difference between winning and losing.

Obama clearly did not have this problem. But Kerry and Hilary did.

And so did Kamala Harris. She did not have what I would call a vision. And while she communicated support for the working class, she did not do a mea culpa or in any way acknowledge that their problems had not been the focus of Democratic policy-making for quite some time.

Now we are in the aftermath of the 2024 election and Democrats must rebuild their base and then expand it. This is not just about winning; it is about saving this country. Independents, the white middle class, Blacks, Latinos, Muslims, and suburban women all

---

[2] Sam Dillon, "War on Terror Dominates Talks Given at Graduations," *The New York Times*, June 12, 2005, p. 28

need to be convinced to vote Democratic; the poor and young who usually don't vote need to be motivated to vote.

To accomplish that, Democrats have to be more than the anti-Trump, especially as Trump is actually ascendent. They must counter the climate of fear, anger and distrust of government [Democrats] that has been fostered by the Republicans, as well as the general apathy of many.

The best way to do this, I believe, is to present a vision for America, and the related policies Democrats propose, that will restore the American people to a feeling of well-being and faith in their and America's future under Democratic leadership. A centrist liberal vision that includes all Americans, that does not pit one segment against another – that speaks to the poor, the middle class, people of all color, and the rich. And this includes corporations; they have a vital role to play, but they cannot be allowed to act against the greater good.

One builds this big tent not by appealing to many separate interests, but by showing people that their interests are not really separate or opposite. That all benefit from liberal policies that move all people and our country forward. Democrats must counter the prevalent us v. them attitude.

Dump identity politics. And create a spirit in which people feel we are all Americans and all are important. This holds true for the middle class and poor who comprise 79% of U.S. households and the top 1% of earners. For White Americans and those of color. Young and old. Urban and rural.

I thus suggest the following Mission Statement for the Democratic Party:

"To build a country of greater opportunity where:
- each and every American has a real chance to experience the promises made in the Declaration of Independence ... 'that *all* men are created equal, that they are endowed by their Creator with certain unalienable Rights ... Life, Liberty, and the pursuit of Happiness;'
- government meets its responsibility as set forth in the Declaration ... 'to secure those rights' ... within the constraints of fiscal responsibility; and

- all citizens have a shared responsibility to support the government's efforts to secure those rights and promote the public good, each according to his ability."

These words from the Declaration of Independence are the moral philosophy, the heart, the soul of American democracy. They are as American as apple pie. This is, or at least until recently was, America's common faith.

In the current debate, Republicans have lost sight of the role of government as stated in the Declaration ... to *secure* the right to life, liberty, and the pursuit of happiness for *all*. And how does government accomplish that? By enacting policies that ensure people have a realistic opportunity to pursue those goals - everyone, not just the poor and disadvantaged, but the middle-class worker as well. What people do with that opportunity is their responsibility.

It is in furtherance of that role that the government acts to protect the public good, create a just society, and build an environment in which people can pursue their right to happiness. It is this aspect of government's role that supports action such as the Clean Air Act and government regulation of business in general.

And it is in furtherance of the American social contract's goal of shared responsibility that we have a system of progressive taxation. The point is not to soak the rich; the point is rather that those who have succeeded can afford to pay a larger share of their income in taxes to support the public good, while those who have not faired well need every dollar to meet the necessities of life.

It is such policies that make the Democratic Party a "life-affirming" force that affirms the profound value of the lives of all living beings. Such policies acknowledge the suffering of millions of citizens caused by their lack of work, stagnant wages, their lack of health insurance, their lack of enough food to eat, or their lack of equal opportunity to acquire a good education ... often simply the result of being born on the "wrong side of the tracks," or losing their job, or facing bankruptcy because of medical bills, or corporate greed – regardless whether White or people of color, urban or rural.

It is such policies that make the Democratic Party a "pro-family" force. How can a family be strong, healthy, and viable without meeting these basic needs?

It is such policies, which respect the value of all human life and the environment, that make the Democratic Party a party of faith – not Christian, not Jewish, not Muslim ... but deep faith. While standing firmly behind the constitutionally mandated separation of church and state, the Democratic Party respects the valued place that religion has had and will always have in the fabric of American life.

By connecting Democratic policy initiatives to our core historic values,[3] *We Still Hold These Truths* presents an overarching vision that will resonate with the American public. Its message is even more urgent now then ever.

But to be successful, the Democrats' vision and policies need to be communicated effectively, in a way the average voter gets. And Democrats must be on the offense, instead of always trying unsuccessfully to counter the negative spin that Republicans have preemptively placed on their policies

As we head into the post-2024 election season and the new Trump administration, it is past time for Democrats to regain the rhetorical upper hand and reclaim their position as the party of the people, the party of America's historic values. And it is past time for Democrats to call the lie to the efforts of the radical Republican movement to portray themselves as anything more than a party supporting the interests of the well-off and big business; we must expose them for what they are ... hypocrites masquerading as the party of the people.

---

[3] Interestingly, in October, 2009 the conservative author and Heritage Foundation fellow Mathew Spalding came out with a book of the same title, *We Still Hold These Truths.* In it he argues that it is the conservative cause that connects to our core historic principles and vilifies progressives, both Democrat and Republican, for perverting those principles. I would respectfully differ.

The 2026 and 2028 elections will once again be the Democrats to lose. Whether they win or lose will be a result of their efforts (or lack thereof) to rebuild their base and the strength or weakness of their campaigns. It is up to them to rouse the people effectively. If they lose it will not be a failure of the people but of the Party.

Ronald Hirsch
December 2024
Washington, Maine

PROLOGUE

"We hold these truths to be self-evident, that all men are created equal, that they are endowed by their Creator with certain unalienable Rights, that among these are Life, Liberty and the pursuit of Happiness.—That to secure these rights, Governments are instituted among Men, deriving their just powers from the consent of the governed . . ."
—Declaration of Independence

THESE WORDS FROM our Declaration of Independence were and remain revolutionary. These words were and remain profoundly liberal, and yet in their interpretation lies the core of both the Liberal and Conservative ideologies that have run through American political life and the tension between them.

Over the past two-hundred-plus years, a system has developed from this liberal foundation that carefully balances rights versus the public good and gives the government an important role in securing individual rights and enforcing public responsibilities. But during the past two decades, and especially under the current Bush administration, a new Republican/Conservative movement has begun to undermine, if not assault, this carefully balanced system and the traditionally liberal American values that underlie it.

- They have favored business/industrial/financial interests over the public interest.
- They have aided the rich while disdaining the poor.
- They have sought to impose the minority moral view of the Religious Right on the entire population through government action.

1

These words from the Declaration also embody a dream, a distinctly American dream, which is central to our Constitution, and comprise the essence of what America is all about . . . and yet despite much progress, it remains a dream for many.

We live in a country of significant and increasing income inequality. According to census figures, while measures of income inequality decreased between 1947 and 1968, since then income inequality has increased, despite the prosperity of the 1990s, to the point where income inequality is now greater than it was in 1947.[1] In other words, the rich have indeed got- ten richer, and the poor have gotten relatively poorer.

- In 2001, the latest year for which such figures are available, the top 20 percent of U.S. households accounted for 50.1 percent of aggregate family income, while the bottom 40 percent accounted for only 12.2 percent of aggregate income (the top's share rose since 1968, while all others dropped).[2]

- The gap was even larger when looking at net worth, with the top 20 percent accounting for 69 percent of aggregate family net worth, and the bottom 40 percent for only 8 percent of net worth. But the problem is not just one of rich versus poor; the middle class (those with incomes in the 40–60 percentile) accounted for only 8 percent of aggregate family net worth.[3]

- While household incomes of the poor and middle class have risen since 1968, those incomes have increased only because women/wives have joined the work force and are working more hours than ever. The average middle-income, two-parent family now works 660 more hours per year—or sixteen more weeks—than in 1979.[4]

- The average American production and nonsupervisory worker's inflation-adjusted weekly wages were actually 5 percent below what they had been in 1973.[5]

An astonishing percentage of the American population is not only poor but living below the government-established poverty line.

- In 2001, 11.7 million children under the age of eighteen, or one out of every six American children, were living below the poverty line, which for a family of three was $14,630. By race and ethnicity, 30 percent of African American children, 28 percent of Hispanic children, 11.5 percent of Asian children, and 9.5 percent of Caucasian children were poor.[6]
- In 2001, 9.2 percent of all families, or 6.8 million families, lived below the poverty level, and 16.6 percent of families with children under six lived below the poverty level.[7]

While it is a given that some percentage of the population will always be very rich and some poor, this magnitude of poverty and income inequality translates to an unacceptable level of inequality in health, in education and in educational opportunity . . . to a lack of equal opportunity to pursue life, liberty, and happiness. It is unacceptable because it demeans the individual and divides our country.

But it is not just with regard to the social issues of poverty and the working poor that the American dream remains just that for many people. Despite decades of laws against discrimination based on sex and race, women and minorities are still often discriminated against in the jobs they get and the incomes they are paid. This basic lack of fairness should be intolerable to every American.

The magnitude and impact of poverty and income inequality, the ongoing discrimination faced by minorities and women, and the divisive policies of the new Republican/Conservative movement—these factors weaken our country. They weaken not only our economic potential, but more importantly, by alienating large masses of the population from the government, they weaken the social fabric, the sense of community that binds us together as a nation.

If government is viewed by a substantial portion of the public as not being a government for *all* the people, including them, then the legitimacy of government is put in question, for as the Declaration says, "to secure these rights, Governments are instituted among Men, deriving their just powers from the consent of the governed."

Using the words of the Declaration as a touchstone, this pamphlet will explore various aspects of American life and government policy to define "an American manifesto." This American manifesto will be true to the liberal roots of this country, to the human progress made under the leadership of Liberals. It will be a resounding call to what remains to be done to make the American dream a reality for all. It will be a resounding call to shape our domestic and foreign policy based on our distinctive American roots. If we succeed, the result will be a stronger, more secure America.

The question is asked frequently, "What does the Democratic Party stand for?" Hopefully, this work will provide the basis for a renewed Democratic ideology rooted in traditional American liberal values, rooted in the Declaration of Independence, yet crafted to meet the needs of our society and economy now and in the future, in a world where many of the assumptions of the past are no longer valid.

Author's Note: Throughout this book, the phrase "Republican/Conservative" is used to refer to adherents of this new Republican/Conservative movement, not Republicans in general, either historically or today, nor traditional Republican Conservatives or Goldwater Conservatives. The phrase Democrats/Liberals is used to refer broadly not just to those who define themselves as Democrats or Liberals, but to all those who consider themselves to be progressives or moderates on public policy issues, regardless of whether they consider themselves affiliated with the Democratic or Republican Party or consider themselves to be Independents.

CHAPTER 1
Federalism and the Protection of Rights
—In the Beginning and Today

My belief has always been . . . that wherever in this land any individual's constitutional rights are being unjustly denied, it is the obligation of the federal government—at point of bayonet if necessary—to restore that individual's constitutional rights.
> —Ronald Reagan, Press Conference, May 17, 1983

[The Bill of Rights] declared in that solemn manner . . . [will] counteract the impulses of interest and passion.
> —James Madison, Madison to Jefferson, October 17, 1788

THE CONSTITUTION'S IMPLEMENTATION of the Declaration of Independence placed emphasis on individual rights and the government's operational framework. In establishing a series of rights or liberties in the Bill of Rights, it was extremely liberal, breaking with established political orthodoxy, and it remains the bedrock of Liberal ideology. Yet, the Bill of Rights at the same time formed the core of Conservative political philoso- phy in that it was about freedom from government intrusion.

But on one important point the Constitution was a conservative document in the sense that it did not break with important established norms of the day—the word "men" was used in a limited sense—free men and biological men; women had no rights, and slavery was allowed as a necessary compromise between the northern and southern states/colonies.

A major issue in creating the new government was the balance of power between the federal government and the states. Ironically, at the time, it was the more liberal and egalitarian party, the Democratic-Republican Party (the party of Thomas

Jefferson, which was derived from the anti-Federalist movement), that was for states' rights and wanted a weak central government. Their focus was on protecting the just-fought-for liberties and involving all the people in government. And it was they who insisted on adding the Bill of Rights to protect those liberties.

Their fear of a strong central government distant from the people was partly in reaction to the Federalist Party, which, in addition to favoring a strong central government, also favored industrial (as opposed to agricultural) interests, control by the upper classes (the educated and wealthy), and a strong military. Although these differences were very strongly felt, the framers of the Constitution were able to find a compromise by wisely striking a balance, creating a strong central government while providing ample room for states' rights and insuring individual rights through the Bill of Rights.

For much of the twentieth century and continuing today, the positions have been reversed; it has been Liberals who have argued for an expanded role for the federal government in protecting individuals and the broader public. They have argued that the federal government must act to protect individual rights guaranteed by the Constitution from state and local government intrusion. They have fought for federal laws to protect consumers, workers, and the public by regulating the most abusive powers of industry. They have supported the fed- eral government's role in securing each person's right to "life, liberty, and the pursuit of happiness" by legislating new rights (for example, Social Security, Medicare, the Americans with Disabilities Act).

Conservatives on the other hand, whether Republican or Democrat, have argued for states' rights and freedom from federal government intrusion in the context of individual rights and civil liberties so that states could be permitted to set their own standards consistent with local mores (for example, racial segregation). On economic issues they generally would prefer no interference from the federal government and so fight to minimize any such interference and support the process of deregulation embraced and accelerated under Rea- gan.

More recently, however, as will be discussed at length in this manifesto, the Republicans/Conservatives have been proactively seeking to use the power of the federal government to weaken constitutional protections, to intrude into certain areas of citizens' personal lives and diminish their individual rights.

The result is that we now have both Liberals and Conservatives arguing for a strong federal stand on certain rights but from diametrically opposed positions. Clearly, Conservatives today do not stand consistently for a small, limited federal government with no federal intrusion into the sphere of individual rights. When it suits their purpose, when they want to limit freedoms, they seek to use the power of the federal government to attain their goals.

Through the decades and centuries, our government has survived because Congress has—with two major exceptions, slavery and the civil war—always been able to find the balance and compromise between the conservative and liberal perspective of those words from the Declaration that was right for the particular point in time.

Beginning with the years of the Clinton administration, however, the Republicans/Conservatives in Congress have taken on a new radical tone, have treated the Democrats/Liberals with vicious derision, and have dropped the history of civility and compromise that has generally enabled both parties to work together. This radicalism and absolutism created legisla- tive gridlock and even threatened to bring the entire government to a halt at one point. While they have strategically backed off somewhat, a basic spirit of intolerance, of self-righteousness, still pervades the Republicans/Conservatives.

This basic issue of the power of government versus the rights of individuals, of the public good versus private rights, often gets resolved by the federal courts, especially the Supreme Court. It is the ultimate check in the system of "checks and balances" created by the framers of the Constitution. It can rule that local, state, or federal government action is unconstitutional, as it did in 1954 in *Brown v. Board of Education*, which found that segregated schools were inherently unequal and thus unconstitutional, and in 1973 in *Roe v. Wade*, which ruled that women had a constitutional right to privacy which included the right to choose whether to have an abortion in the early stages of pregnancy.

Given the power of the courts, it should come as no surprise that presidents tend to nominate judges who agree with or are sympathetic to their view of government and the Constitution. Since Republican presidents have been in office for fifteen of the last twenty-three years, they have appointed a total of 724 federal judges, including 152 appeals' court and 5 Supreme Court judges. Clinton, during his eight years in office, appointed a total of 374 judges, including 66 appeals' court, and 2 Supreme Court judges. The numbers tell why, today, there is often a conservative majority on the Supreme Court as well as on many of the appeals' courts.

Perhaps the most vivid example of the impact of the appointment power was President George H. W. Bush's decision to fill the Supreme Court seat vacated by Thurgood Marshall, a leader of the civil rights movement in the 1950s, a staunch liberal, and an eminent lawyer, jurist, and solicitor general, with Clarence Thomas, an opponent of affirmative action, a staunch conservative, and a lawyer and jurist of little note.

While the Republican focus is often on the importance of overturning *Roe v. Wade*, the negative impact of a strongly conservative majority on the Supreme Court and on the appellate courts would extend into all areas of government policy and action, including the environment, civil rights, and securi- ty.

A central issue that gives rise to the danger of a strongly conservative majority is whether the Constitution would then be interpreted in a "strict constructionist" manner. Our nation has survived as a democracy in part because the courts have treated the Constitution as a living document. They have recognized that it was a reflection of the mores at a point in time and that the interpretation of its words, as opposed to the basic framework, legitimately can and even must change as the social and political context changes for the governmental system to survive and reflect "the consent of the governed." A strict constructionist does not agree that there is such flexibility.

To prevent the Republicans/Conservatives from completing their takeover of the federal judicial system and implementing their conservative agenda, the Democratic candidate for president must win in 2004 and the Democrats must re- gain control of the Senate. To accomplish this, Demo- crats/Liberals must not only rally the populace to the urgency of this particular issue but also follow the suggestions made in the following chapters to reconnect with the American people. They must reclaim the Declaration of Independence and the Constitution as essentially liberal documents and stake their claim as the party of democracy. The bluster and hypocrisy of the Republicans/Conservatives must be exposed for what it is, a spirit whose character runs counter to America's historic values and the essence of our founding documents.

CHAPTER 2
The American Social Contract

Government of the people, by the people, and for the people . . .
—Abraham Lincoln, Speech, November 19, 1863

THESE IMMORTAL WORDS from Abraham Lincoln's *Gettysburg Address* describe very simply the American social contract, the relationship between the citizen and our government and the responsibilities of both.

As the nature of the body politic and its political views changed during the course of the nineteenth century, there was a shift from the philosophy that each man was his own master and whether he succeeded or failed in the new egalitarian society it was to his credit or fault. The new philosophy instead recognized that many individuals were impacted by society-driven factors over which they had no control and which had a significantly negative effect on their ability to make the most of their lives.

Especially after 1890, the reform movement gained strength, fueled by the extremes of poverty and wealth found in the country, as well as the general population's dislike of what it saw as the absolute power of big business, corruption scandals in government, and the violent suppression of strikes. The result over the next few decades was an American social contract with increasing emphasis on a balance of rights and individual obligations, and the role of government in leveling the playing field, with each person contributing to the gov- ernment's support according to his ability.

During this period the views of Liberals and Conservatives on social policy and the role of government became even more ideologically distinct. Conservatives continued to champion the rights of the establishment, of business/industrial interests, of property. They interpreted individual freedoms narrowly if they went against those rights. Liberals, on the other hand, championed the new immigrant classes, the new laboring class created by the industrial revolution, the emerging middle class, and the necessary role of government in securing their rights to "life, liberty, and the pursuit of happiness."

Ultimately, due to the opening of the vote to all men of age and later to women, and because of the changing demographics of the country, the Liberal perspective increasingly carried the day in the political arena and in the judicial arena as well. In the early 1900s, and indeed throughout much of the twentieth century, that Liberal perspective was well represented in both the Republican and Democratic parties. Indeed it was Theodore Roosevelt, a liberal Republican, who called for a "square deal for all Americans," supported miners in a strike by forcing the mine owners to the bargaining table, and gained fame as a "trust buster" by breaking up some of the largest and most influential trusts in the country, such as the Standard Oil Trust.

Later, FDR's New Deal and Lyndon Johnson's Great Society expanded the role of government under the American social contract in securing the right to life, liberty, and the pursuit of happiness for the elderly, the poor, and minorities. The legislation that established Social Security, Medicare, and federal protection from discrimination had a major impact, together with other legislation of the period, in improving the health and financial security for millions of Americans.

Today, matters that were once anathema to Conservatives would never be questioned. Their foundation as part of the American social contract, whether through legislation or judicial interpretation, is too well-established. Through political compromise and balance, the rights of both citizens and business interests have been protected, with none having absolute freedom of action and all contributing through taxes to support government in securing our inalienable rights. But, as will be argued throughout this manifesto, the new Republican/Conservative radicalism is threatening that balance on many fronts.

Key to the legitimacy of government under the Declaration, the Constitution, and the American social contract, indeed to the survival of this country, is the consent and active involvement of the governed. Yet over the past three decades, there has developed an increasing distance and ambivalence between a large segment of the population and the government as evidenced most vividly in the declining percentage of individuals who vote. (The following figures are from the Federal Election Commission.[8])

- In the presidential elections of 1960, 1964, and1968, voter turnout ranged between 61 and 63 percent of the voting-age population (VAP), and between 90 and 95 percent of registered voters voted.
- In the presidential elections since 1972, voter turnout has dropped to between 49 and 55 percent of the VAP, and the percentage of registered voters voting dropped steadily from 80 percent in 1972 to only 67 percent in 1996 and 2000.

Why did this happen? Part of this is a matter of demographics . . . the increasing disparity between the rich and the poor, between CEOs and workers, the cycle of poverty and violence that has trapped the poor. Part of it is a result of the Vietnam War, because the government was viewed by many as being unresponsive to their view that this war was unnecessary and wrong; they felt their voice was callously ignored. Part of it stems from the disgrace of Watergate and the general lack of trust in politicians because of the influence of "special interests" and in particular large corporations. For many, the government seems out of touch with the people and their needs. It seems almost irrelevant to their daily lives.

Part of this mood of alienation also comes from the "me" generation that was borne of Ronald Reagan. That phenomenon resulted in weakening the sense of community that is an essential part of the American social contract. How different from the call in John F. Kennedy's inaugural address, "Ask not what your country can do for you—ask what you can do for your country."

But part of this also results from the general absence of strong personalities, leaders, and speakers among the Democrats/Liberals . . . a failure of Liberals to connect to their roots and delineate and communicate issues strongly and effectively to the body politic. Starting with Ronald Reagan's "there he goes again" during the Reagan/Carter Presidential debates, the Republicans/Conservatives have been successful at ridiculing Democrats/Liberals and philosophically emasculating them. They have allowed Republicans/Conservatives to define what a "liberal" is in the minds of the public, and that definition is not a moderate or centrist but rather a radical left-winger, a person out of step with the American people. Clinton was able to break this trend partly because of his strong rhetorical skills and presence, his ability to communicate his positions and is- sues and connect with people.

At the same time, the Republicans/Conservatives have become the firebrands, the forceful voices with a vision, of the latter part of the twentieth century and early twenty-first century. This boldness has appealed to the citizenry because the citizenry equates boldness with leadership. Thus, through a combination of strong personas, boldness, and the denigration of Liberals, the Republican Party has been able to position itself in the minds of many as the party of common sense and bedrock Americanism, and so has been very effective at rousing and expanding its political base. This, despite the fact that many Republican/Conservative positions are radical, in that they are out of step with the centrist mainstream of the popu- lation.

The impact of the withdrawal of many traditional Democrats from the active voting base together with the revitalization and expansion of the Republican base, largely due to the fervor of the Religious Right, is shown in recent polls by both the Gallup Organization[9] and the Harris Poll.[10] Both show that the Democrats have lost the strong edge in voter identifi- cation that they had held for many years. The Gallup poll found that equal numbers of Americans identified themselves as Democrats and Republicans, a loss of a 9 percent lead in just the past decade. The Harris poll found the Democrats reduced to a 3 percent lead in voter identification, the lowest since it began measuring voter identification in 1969.

Democrats/Liberals must boldly stand up for their principles and their causes.

- They must reconnect to their roots in the Declaration of Independence and the Constitution.
- They must be champions of the American worker and the nonrich with a clear message of both the rights and obligations of all, while being supportive of the growth of business and industry.
- They must, as noted by Ted Halstead in *The Atlantic*,[11] seek new ways to ensure the economic fairness and equal opportunity that is central to the American social contract while allowing the flexibility that is ne-

cessary in the post-industrial age, thus adapting the American social contract to the new conditions we face.

- They must rekindle a sense of community and common purpose among our diverse population by working with the leadership of all segments of our society. The prevalence of an "us versus them" perspective, of the self-absorption of the "me" mentality, must be replaced with a realization that we are all in many ways dependent on one another. The increasing divisions within our nation must be narrowed.

- They must reshape in the mind of the American public the meaning and connotation of the word "liberal" which has been hijacked and distorted by Republicans/Conservatives. To be a Liberal is not to be a radical or a left-winger. Rather, a Liberal in the American context is a centrist, true to the values and principles that at the core of America's founding documents.

The issue is not big government versus small government, high taxes versus low taxes. The issue is what must the role of government be in order to live up to those words in the Declaration and what is the role of each of us under the American social contract. The issue is saving America from a conservative radicalism on economic, environmental, social, and moral fronts.

The current generation of Republicans/Conservatives want freedom from government intrusion in matters that impact how businesses operate, and yet they support government in- trusion into some of the most private areas of human life. These policies are interest driven and ideologically inconsis- tent. Even stalwart conservatives of the old school, like Barry Goldwater, have clearly stated their disagreement with this support of government intrusion fostered by the Religious Right. Further, Republicans/Conservatives do not strongly support and in some cases oppose the government's role in leveling the playing field for all. The combination of these policies is destructive of the American social contract and contrary to the spirit of the Declaration and Constitution. These policies weaken the country.

Democrats/Liberals must challenge those policies by arguing that the American social contract and the liberal philosophy underlying it implies that rights, whether economic or personal, should be free from government intrusion except where the exercise of those rights would harm another individual or where a limitation on those rights is necessary to protect the greater good.

They must expose the hypocrisy of the Republicans/Conservatives . . . wanting the federal government to stay out of business affairs and not interfere in a state's view of local civil-rights mores regardless of the greater public good, yet wanting the power of the federal government to intrude on the most personal and private areas of citizens' lives in order to impose the tenets of a minority religious movement on the majority.

Ultimately, Democrats/Liberals must argue that the role of government under the American social contract is "to secure the right" to life, liberty, and the pursuit of happiness, and that government therefore must act to regulate business/industry and to provide those not born of privilege a real equality of opportunity so that they can fairly exercise their rights.

CHAPTER 3
Religion, Morality, and the State

I believe in an America where the separation of church and state is absolute. I believe in an America that is officially neither Catholic, Protestant nor Jewish—where no public official either requests or accepts instructions on public policy from [any] ecclesiastical source—where no religious body seeks to impose its will directly or indirectly upon the general populace or the public acts of its officials.
        —John F. Kennedy, Speech, September 12, 1960

FROM ITS COLONIAL ORIGINS onward, the United States has been a country whose citizens have held deeply felt religious beliefs. Those beliefs have rooted Americans in numerous ways, including providing a system of moral values. It is natu- ral that those beliefs and the morality that flows from those beliefs impact public policy, and it has from the time of the Declaration of Independence to the present day. Indeed, the words from the Declaration quoted at the beginning of this manifesto say that these unalienable rights are "endowed by their Creator."

But from the time of the founding fathers, there has been a recognition enshrined in our Constitution that there is no one "right" approach to God, no one "true" religion, that there are many religions and indeed many denominations within each religion, each of whom has sought their own way to approach God. Each of those religions and denominations, in turn, has established norms of behavior which flow from their specific creed, and these norms, in their specifics, vary greatly one from the other, even within the same religion.

The founding fathers were well aware of the problems caused in Europe by enshrining a state's largely shared religious belief as the state religion. The result was the official persecution of religious minorities in those countries, not just Jews and other "unbelievers" but even Christians such as the Eng- lish Puritans, the Dutch Calvinists, or the German Menno- nites. They were also familiar with the wars that had been fought in the name of religion.

They were also aware that some of those persecuted minorities who came to these shores for freedom sought only freedom for themselves and their creed. They replaced the intolerance of the state religion of the old country with their own state religion and intolerance and persecution of those within their communities who strayed from the doctrinally dictated religious path.

Determined that such problems of divisiveness and persecution not be present in this new egalitarian country, and understanding the importance and the personal nature of one's religious beliefs, the founding fathers included, in the Bill of Rights as the First Amendment, the following: "Congress shall make no law respecting an establishment of religion, or prohibiting the free exercise thereof." This is the language that created the joint concepts of freedom of religion and the separation of church and state. As an aside, it is interesting to note that while the Declaration is based on rights from "the Creator," the word "God" or "Creator" is not to be found in the Preamble or elsewhere in the Constitution. We are, as has often been said, a country governed by the laws of man, not the laws of God.

And so the United States is not a Christian country, although Christians may form the majority of the population and Judeo-Christian beliefs may permeate much of our government policy. It then is certainly not a Protestant, Catholic, Presbyterian, or Evangelical country. Of key importance to the maintenance of this freedom is the principle that the power of the state must not, through legislation or otherwise, support the tenets of one religion or denomination over those of another. When government adopts policies that favor and im- pose the viewpoint of one religious group over another as well as over the broader morality of the general populace, then such action would be tantamount to the government "making a law respecting an establishment of religion," which is prohibited by the First Amendment to the Constitution.

During the two-hundred-plus years of this country, re- gardless of the religious affiliation or beliefs (or lack thereof) of the president or members of Congress, there has been a rather scrupulous separation of any one specific religious doctrine from the laws and policies of this country. There are formulaic recognitions of the basic religious beliefs of the population, such as the reference in the Pledge of Allegiance to one nation "under God." And there are references to God and to Chris- tianity in political oratory, perhaps none more elegant that William Jennings Bryan's cry, "You shall not crucify labor on a cross of gold." And certainly the shared morality found in all religions forms the basis for many of our social policies.

But the tenets of a specific religion have not intruded into the secular realm of our laws. When John F. Kennedy ran for president, one of the greatest fears of many Protestants was that the president, as a Catholic, would listen to or be con- trolled by the pope in his development of legislation and poli- cy, both domestic and international. That fear was, of course, unfounded.

During the past two decades or so, however, what is often referred to as "the Religious Right" has become an ever more prominent voice within the Republican Party. At the 1992 Republican Convention, it was a major presence, seizing con- trol of that part of the Republican platform and agenda that related to its core concerns and solidifying its conservative religious influence on the rest of the party.

On issues ranging from homosexuality and the concept of gay rights to a woman's right to choose abortion to HIV sex education, the Religious Right has sought to impose its particular view of Christian morality on the entire populace through government action or inaction. In this and in their fervor and self-righteousness, they are not much different from the radical Islamists who seek to replace secular governments with ones that are ruled by religious law.

During the current Bush administration, this distinctly minority viewpoint has finally succeeded in finding a kindred spirit in the White House and has managed to exert an influence and control which has led to the adoption of various government policies or inaction, as will be discussed in detail later in this book, that directly affect the lives of millions of Americans.

The Constitution was meant to protect minorities from the tyranny of the majority. How ironic it would be if the Re-ligious Right minority were able to exercise tyranny over the majority by having its tenets imposed by the government on the entire population.

Democrats/Liberals must protect the country from this tyranny of the minority by rousing the majority, regardless of party affiliation, whether liberal, moderate, or conservative, to speak with a common voice against this abridgment of their rights. Such action is not antireligious, nor is it against any particular religion. The efforts in July 2003 by Republicans/Conservatives on the Senate Judiciary Committee to cast opposition to pro-life judicial nominations as being anti-Catholic, for example, are not just ludicrous (especially given that the pro-life senators in question were Protestants, and the pro-choice senators were Catholics) but extremely divisive.

Rather the purpose of such opposition is to enforce the First Amendment and ensure that the morality that is enshrined in our laws is a morality that is supported by the broad base of religions and the populace of this country.

Religion has had and will always have a valued and important place as part of the fabric of American life. Those who bemoan the lack of moral values in much of our population today have a valid point to make . . . many have little respect for themselves and for others. Religion can and hopefully will play an important role in reestablishing traditional American moral values and feelings of community through the power of the pulpit and its relationship with its believers, but not through the power of the government. Church and state must remain separate.

CHAPTER 4
Education

A mind is a terrible thing to waste.®

—United Negro College Fund

IF A CHILD DOES NOT have equal opportunity in education, then that child will not have an equal opportunity to obtain jobs, financial security and well-being. And without that, the right to life, liberty, and the pursuit of happiness is an emptier one. So central is this issue. Of the many factors one could dis- cuss that impact the quality of educational opportunity, two of the more vital factors are equality in the funding of primary and secondary education and the availability of early childhood education.

We live in a society where the quality of public education one receives is a direct consequence of the wealth of the school district in which one resides; the resulting disparities are large. According to figures from the National Center for Education Statistics, school districts in poorer areas (with 25 percent or more students living in poverty) have 20 percent less funds to spend per pupil on average than districts within wealthier areas (with 5 percent or fewer students living in poverty) . . . and this is after factoring in differences in cost of living and accounting for supplementation from federal and state budgets.[12]

What does this mean in practical terms? Working from the median expenditure per pupil figure for the 1998–99 school year of $6,110[13] (with the range being from an unadjusted low of $4,210 for Utah, and a high of $10,145 for New Jersey), it means that a district with a better income base would have on average roughly $1,300–1,500 more available per pupil (after accounting for cost of living) than a school district with a higher incidence of poverty.

Now that may not sound like a big difference, but considering a classroom size of thirty students, that translates to a $39,000–45,000 per year difference *per classroom*. Think what a difference that would make whether through higher teacher salaries to attract better teachers, more and better equipment, teacher assistants, better maintenance, etc.

Regardless of whether one considers this inequality to be unconstitutional or not, it is unacceptable in today's America and weakens the American social contract. Not only is it de- structive for individuals born in a less advantageous situation, relegating them to a life without real options, but it is also very harmful to the American economy which is ever more depen- dent on a well-educated work force. Enlightened self-interest, if nothing else, argues in favor of the government's responsibility for providing equality of education funding.

The answer, however, does not lie in merely pooling property taxes and redistributing them on a per-pupil basis, thus in effect dumbing down the quality of education received in the suburbs. Rather, additional funds must be provided.

The answer lies in increasing the funding received from state and/or federal sources by school districts in inner cities and areas of rural poverty and improving the quality of educa- tion in those districts with such funds. Those funds may come, as was recently suggested in an *Atlantic* article by Mathew Mil- ler (July/August 2003 issue), by having the federal government augment teachers' salaries in urban school districts, or by some other means, including new or increased taxes at the state level. Yes, this will probably require new money rather than the shift- ing of resources, but there are few matters more critical to our country's future. The time is long since past that the quality of education was a strictly local issue; it is an issue of major national importance.

But the process of education and development does not start at age four when a child enters kindergarten. The years prior to that are very important, especially so for children living in poverty. Children in this society are not born equal in the sense that they are born into very different circumstances . . . to parents of vastly varying educational accomplishments or intel- ligence, of vastly varying degrees of interest in their children's education, and vastly varying wealth . . . and they grow up in social environments that vary greatly in the value they place on education. These differences significantly impact the development of a child. Children living in poverty need a head start, and so the government provides many such children early childhood education through the aptly named Head Start pro- gram.

There is no question of the benefits derived from the program. Studies of both the Head Start program and of Early Head Start, which was enacted in 1994 to support infants, tod- dlers, and their families, have found that participants' learning skills and cognitive and socio-emotional development improved compared to students who didn't participate, and that they were therefore more likely to succeed in school. In addition, studies of the Early Head Start program found that parents in- volved in the program had more positive parenting behavior, used physical punishment less often, and were more likely to provide help to their children at home.[14]

Despite a proven track record and a proven need, however, Head Start still only has the funding to reach about three out of five eligible preschool-age children. Despite the importance of Early Head Start, it only reaches approximately 50,000 infants and toddlers out of over 2 million eligible children.[15] Both these programs need to be expanded so that every child in America has access to early childhood education.

Yet, equality of education funding and early childhood education cannot, in and of themselves, achieve the desired change in educational opportunity. What is needed in addition is a secure school environment, and an environment in which excelling in education is valued and there is more parent involvement. These are not matters that can be accomplished through government fiat. Rather, these are objectives which government, civic, and religious leaders must all join together to achieve.

It is common for politicians of all stripes, Republican and Democrat, Liberal and Conservative, to say that the hope of our country lies in our children. But talk is cheap. The time has come for Democrats/Liberals to emphasize that our hope lies in *all* of our children, and for government, joined by civic and religious leaders and the entire populace, to work together to insure that no child in this great and prosperous country of ours is denied an equal opportunity to make the most of his or her God-given talents.

CHAPTER 5
Health Care

[The Declaration] prescribed the proper role of government, . . . to ef-
fect [individuals'] safety and happiness. In modern society, no individ-
ual can do this alone. So government is not a necessary evil but a neces-
sary good.

—Gerald R. Ford, Speech, July 4, 1976

HEALTH IS MORE IMPORTANT to people than almost any other
factor in their lives. Children need good nutrition and health in
order to be able to learn. Adults need good health in order to
lead productive lives and earn a living. Seniors need good health
in order to remain independent. Without health, life and liberty
have less quality and the pursuit of happiness has less meaning.
And as with education, a healthy population is also important to
the health of our economy in many ways.

Health care thus has long been an important priority of our
government, and huge sums are paid through Medicare and
Medicaid to provide health care to the poor and the elder- ly.
Other government programs provide needed nutrition assistance to families, children, and pregnant women living in poverty.

But there remain serious gaps. According to data from the
Census Bureau,[16] in 2001,

- The number of people who had no health insurance was
  41.2 million, or 14.6 percent of the population. Of
  those, 8.5 million were children.
- Despite the Medicaid program, 10.1 million poor
  people, or 30.7 percent of the poor, had no health insurance of any kind in 2001.

- Approximately 33 million people (nearly 11 percent of U.S. households) were food insecure, meaning that they did not have adequate access to enough food for a healthy, active life. Of those, roughly 6 million were children.[17]

In a country as rich as the United States, the fact that 41 million of our citizens have no health insurance, the fact that 33 million people do not have enough to eat, is unacceptable.

Many other countries provide all their citizens with health insurance. Providing universal health insurance in the United States, however, has become a highly charged political issue. Why? Because it is anathema to the insurance industry (most plans are government plans, not privatized ones) and Conservatives (it's an example of big government that will cause tax increases), and they together have created among the people a fear on this issue borne of confusion and loss of choice. They have successfully portrayed this as an example of big government interfering in people's lives.

Democrats/Liberals must seize on this issue again and place it in its proper perspective. This is not an example of the menace of big government, as portrayed in the infamous "Har- ry and Louise" issue ads paid for by the insurance industry at the time of the fight over the Clinton administration's plan for universal health coverage. Rather, this is a solid example of the correct role of government under the American social contract. The government has a duty to secure the right of those less fortunate to life, liberty, and the pursuit of happiness. Beyond providing for the poor, national health insurance would help relieve the stress that many families feel due to the loss of long- term job security in today's economy. This is not just govern- ment helping people; it is government working to make our country stronger for the greater public good.

While it may certainly be true that some of the existing universal health-care systems have their drawbacks, and while the system proposed by the Clinton administration was flawed, those are lessons we can learn from. They are not reasons not to move forward.

For example, the English system may involve some rationing of health care, but that does not mean that our system would have that feature, which Americans fear and want no part of. Instead, cost savings could come from omitting "excess" care. According to the Center for Evaluative Clinical Sciences at Dartmouth Medical School, "20 to 30 percent of health-care spending goes for procedures, drugs, hospitaliza- tion . . . that do absolutely nothing to improve the quality or increase the length of our lives."[18]

The time is ripe to address this issue again, given the re- cent publication of an article in *JAMA* by the Physicians Working Group (a group of eight thousand physicians and medical students) proposing a single-payer national health in- surance for all.[19] Whether this plan is adopted or one of the other approaches that have been suggested, providing health insurance for all Americans is critical to the health of our citizens and the health of our economy.

Beyond the issue of universal health-insurance coverage and broader nutrition assistance, there is an urgent need for the details of health programs and health policy, especially in the areas of HIV and family planning, to be removed from the ever more pervasive influence and control of the Religious Right.

The spread of HIV in our country remains a major problem. There are approximately forty thousand new cases of HIV each year. The epidemic increasingly affects women, minorities, persons infected through heterosexual contact, and the poor,[20] with women accounting for one-third of new HIV cases in 2001. HIV in youth, and especially in minority youth, is also a major problem.[21] HIV's main method of transmission is through sex.

Absent a cure or vaccine, our only way of combating HIV is through effective prevention programs. The goal of these programs in the past has been to reduce or eliminate specific at-risk sexual behavior (often through a frank discussion of the facts and the distribution of free condoms), not to stop sexual activity. It is the Religious Right's position, however, that the goal must be to stop "inappropriate" (homosexual or premarital) sex by teaching abstinence and that education on condom use should not be condoned because it would encourage sexual activity. The impact of this position on the Bush administration and Republicans in Congress can be seen in the following examples:

- In April 2003, the CDC announced a new direction in tackling the HIV epidemic, which moves away from community outreach to noninfected individuals and the free distribution of condoms to encourage safe-sex behavior.[22] While the new emphasis on counseling infected individuals is needed, abandoning outreach to those not infected is a recipe for disaster.

- As reported in the *New York Times*, prevention researchers recently have been warned by federal health officials that their research may come under unusual scrutiny by the Department of Health and Human Services or by members of Congress because the topics are politically controversial. To avoid such scrutiny they have been advised to avoid using any of the fol- lowing words in their applications: gay, homosexual, anal sex, men who have sex with men, needle exchange and sex workers.[23] How can one study HIV prevention without referring to such basic aspects of the HIV epidemic? A sadder example of burying one's face in the sand does not exist.

- One-third of the funds used to combat the spread of HIV in Africa under the new U.S. aid effort are restricted to abstinence-only programs as a result of pressure on congressmen from the Family Research Council, among others.[24]

In areas of the country where the Religious Right is a major political force, high-school sex-education programs cannot discuss HIV prevention in any other terms than abstinence. Now, while teaching abstinence to teenagers is definitely a worthwhile element and should even be a central part of sex education, it is bad public policy and foolhardy not to understand that many youth will ignore that message. To protect them and to protect the broader public, it is critically impor- tant that they receive information about various forms of safe sex and condom use. This is the position voiced by the Bush administration's own surgeon general, Dr. Richard Carmona, who has advocated comprehensive sex education that includes both condom use and abstinence.[25]

Another example lies in the area of family planning. In much of the underdeveloped world, rampant birthrates are a major problem in efforts by those countries to improve their economies and decrease the extent of poverty. Family-planning programs often provide information on early term abortion, as well as various forms of contraception, to empower women to limit the size of their families.

Yet the Religious Right, in its zealotry to eliminate abortion everywhere regardless of the resulting devastating impact, influenced the Reagan administration to enact a rule that prohibits funding from U.S. agencies to any programs that include abortion counseling as part of family planning, regardless of whether abortion is legal in that country and regardless if U.S. funds are not used for that purpose.[26] President Bush reinstated this rule on his second day in office.

Democrats/Liberals must fight to return these areas of public-health policy to the domain of science and rational thought and free these policies, and the millions impacted by these policies, from this usurpation of government policy by the Religious Right.

CHAPTER 6
Civil Rights

I have a dream that one day this nation will rise up and live out the true meaning of its creed: 'We hold these truths to be self-evident: that all men are created equal.' . . . And when this happens, When we al- low freedom to ring, . . . we will be able to speed up that day when all of God's children, black men and white men, Jews and Gentiles, Prot- estants and Catholics, will be able to join hands and sing in the words of the old Negro spiritual, 'Free at last! Free at last! Thank God Al- mighty, we are free at last!'

—Martin Luther King, Jr., March on Washington,
August 28, 1963

THE CONCEPT OF LIBERTY, of individual civil rights, is the cornerstone of the Declaration and the Constitution. As the United States has evolved over the past two-hundred-plus years, that concept of liberty and civil rights has slowly ex- panded to include an ever broader segment of the population and a broader range of human activity.

The Constitution extended the vote to all free men (in the colonies, only men of property could vote). Lincoln's Emanci- pation Proclamation freed the slaves and in 1870, with the ratification of the Fifteenth Amendment, the states were pro- hibited from denying voting rights based on race. In 1920, women were given the right to vote with the ratification of the Nineteenth Amendment.

But the right to vote, while important, does not guarantee equality of opportunity or freedom from discrimination in many facets of life (education, housing, the workplace, public accommodations, and even voting). Securing freedom from discrimination and equal opportunity came to be seen as an essential part of the government's role in securing the right of all to life, liberty, and the pursuit of happiness.

The process began with President Truman's appointment of a President's Committee on Civil Rights in 1947 and his executive order ending segregation in the armed services in 1948. It continued with the landmark case of *Brown v. Board of Education* (1954), which held that separate segregated educational facilities are inherently unequal and thus unconstitutional.

Since then, the federal government has sought to protect people from discrimination on the basis of race, sex, religion, ethnicity, national origin, and, more recently, disability through executive action and legislation. It has taken executive action to enforce court orders (for example, when President Eisenhower sent the National Guard to enforce court-ordered school integration in Little Rock, Arkansas in 1957). And, it has enacted a series of legislation, especially the Civil Rights Act of 1964. The groups protected have all been groups for whom the history of discrimination was systematic and well- documented.

Yet despite the legislation and many court decisions, the factors of race and sex in particular, as well as disability, continue to be the cause of systematic and widespread discrimination, less blatant than previously perhaps, but nevertheless effective. As long as this continues, our nation will never be, as we say in the Pledge of Allegiance, "one Nation under God, indivisible, with liberty and justice *for all*."

What is needed to end discrimination is not more laws or more court decisions. What is needed is a call by government, civic, business, and religious leaders that discrimination must end at all levels and in all its forms. A new peer pressure must be created that does not condone discrimination and that permeates all areas of society. Racial jokes may not be "politically correct" in our society, but discrimination under the table is still acceptable and certainly not uncommon practice.

Only Democrats/Liberals can legitimately take this leadership role. Republican tactics of the past decades, and as recently as December 2002 when Republican Senate Majority Leader Trent Lott praised Strom Thurmond's segregationist Dixiecrat presidential campaign of 1948, show that the Republicans/Conservatives are tainted by their history of race baiting and less than full-hearted support, if not opposition to, many issues impacting women.

But there remains one group historically subject to widespread and systematic discrimination and violence which is still largely unprotected by the law—gays and lesbians. At one point, the argument was that homosexuals choose their status, and so they are different from the classifications of race or sex. But, it is now generally accepted by scientists that homosexual- ity results from a combination of genetics and environment, not individual choice. Further, the American Psychiatric Association removed homosexuality from the list of psychiatric disorders thirty years ago.

As a result of the increasing public recognition that homosexuality is a "status," like race and sex, and that gays and lesbians are a healthy part of our society, 14 states and 240 localities have passed laws over the past twenty years that prohibit discrimination in employment based on sexual orientation. But, such a law has remained elusive at the national level, ex- cept through a Clinton-administration executive order that applies to all federal employees.

Interestingly, while the federal government was ahead of the general population in its call for an end to discrimination based on race, with regards to gays and lesbians, it would ap- pear from consistent poll data and the actions of many businesses and religious groups that the populace is ahead of Congress and the president. For example:

- The Harris Poll found in 2001 that by more than two to one (from 61–20 percent and 58–29 percent), most Americans support a federal law to prohibit job discrimination against gays and lesbians.[27]
- In April 2003, the Harris Poll found that 82 percent were against state laws that regulate private consensual sexual conduct of same-sex adult couples. "Across the board, regardless of income, gender, age, region of the country, or political philosophy, Americans overwhelmingly oppose state laws that regulate sexual relations that occur in the private home of an adult same-sex couple." That survey also found that an overwhelming majority, 76 percent, opposes denying someone in a same-sex relationship certain jobs such as teaching.[28]
- An August, 2003 bipartisan poll, conducted by the Democratic polling firm of Peter D. Hart Research Associates and the Republican firm American Viewpoint, showed that 63 percent of registered voters support or accept equal rights for gays and lesbians.[29]
- The fact that 373 of the Fortune 500 companies, including family-oriented Walmart, and a total of 2,967 employers across the country have adopted nondiscrimination policies that include sexual orientation[30] shows the broad support that the proposition—that gays and lesbians should be treated as equals—has in the general population.

In the recent U.S. Supreme Court case of *Lawrence v. Tex- as* (2003), which struck down a Texas law making same-sex sodomy a crime, Justice Kennedy reflected this changed context when he wrote for the majority that, "The Nation's laws and traditions. . . show an emerging awareness that liberty gives substantial protection to adult persons in deciding how to conduct their private lives in matters pertaining to sex. . . . This Court's obligation is to define the liberty of all, not to mandate its own moral code."[31]

Why then is Congress out of step with the American public, as well as with most of the developed world, on this issue? The answer, once again, is that the Religious Right has captured the conservative movement and the Republican Party, and its view of morality has become the Republican view.

A vivid and public example of the hold of the Religious Right on the Republican Party occurred at the 1992 Republican National Convention. In a primetime speech,[32] archconservative Pat Buchanan made the now-famous statement, "There is a religious war going on in our country for the soul of America. It is a cultural war . . ."

He said that on the one side are those who are pro-life, for strict-constructionist judges, and "against the amoral idea that gay and lesbian couples should have the same standing in law as married men and women." He characterized those on the other side as supporters of "radical feminism. The agenda Clinton & Clinton would impose on America—abortion on demand . . . homosexual rights . . . that's change, all right. But it is not the kind of change America wants . . . And it is not the kind of change we can tolerate in a nation that we still call God's country."

How self-righteous of him to speak for what the nation can tolerate, even for what religious clergy can tolerate.

- In August 2003, the Episcopal Church of the United States' House of Bishops formally approved the appointment of an openly gay priest to be bishop of New Hampshire by a vote of 62–45.[33]

- Concerned Clergy of West Michigan, in responding to many churches' homophobia and exclusion, say, "We see it as a misinterpretation of the gospel's call for the church to be the 'body of Christ'" and contrary to "Jesus' radical ethic of inclusive love." They say that accepting same-sex unions does not threaten the validity of heterosexual marriage.[34]

- The Religious Coalition for the Freedom to Marry, a group of more than 450 clergy from over a dozen different faith traditions based in Boston, have stated their belief in the "inherent right of gay and lesbian couples to be given the rights, protections and legal responsibilities under the law" that are given to married couples, while leaving the decision on religious marriage to the various religious communities.[35]

However, in the latter part of 2003, various polls indicated a public backlash to the concept of gay "marriage." This, together with the strong advocacy of the Religious Right, has led President Bush to support a constitutional amendment to define marriage as between a man and a woman. This is a drastic and ill-advised measure that, according to an ABC News/Washington Post Poll conducted just days prior to the 2004 State of the Union message, is not even supported by a majority of Republicans.[36] Many state legislatures are considering similar measures in order to prohibit same-sex marriages.

Gay "marriage" has quickly become a hot-button issue, which is galvanizing the Religious Right and Republicans/Conservatives and is discomforting to many who otherwise support gay rights. It thus threatens to have a major impact on the 2004 election and warrants careful analysis.

The public's problem lies not in the concept of same-sex civil unions, but in the word "marriage," because of its religious connotation. While the concept of same-sex "marriage" clearly is not generally accepted by the public, the concept of civil unions with attendant legal rights is another matter. A January 2004 USAToday/CNN/Gallup Poll showed that while 53 percent oppose allowing same-sex couples to get mar- ried, only 41 percent oppose laws that allow the formation of civil unions with various legal rights of married couples.[37]

Why this substantial difference in result? I suggest that when this and other polls have asked questions regarding same- sex marriage, the respondents think the question is about reli- gious marriage. The poll results, however, have been used by the Religious Right and Republicans/Conservatives to say that the public is against civil marriage, which of course is the only form of marriage within the government's jurisdiction. This interpretation of the data is without justification.

A more reasonable interpretation, given the public's gener- al support of gay rights, is that people see a major distinction between same-sex *religious* marriage, which for many would infringe on their religious beliefs, and *civil* union/marriage which is wholly a secular matter. The various polls, therefore, do not show that the public is against same-sex *civil* marriage. I believe that a review of the polls relating to gay and lesbian rights issues show that for the majority of Americans, there is no culture war; instead, there is tolerance.

Democrats/Liberals must make this distinction clear in the public debate. They must also make clear that providing for same-sex civil marriage would have no impact on the freedom of religions to refuse to marry same-sex couples; under the First Amendment, that is within their province to decide. When the public realizes that only civil marriage is on the ta- ble, the emotionalism generated by that word will be defused, and reason and fairness will prevail; the tide will shift to public support for same-sex civil marriage. There is no valid reason to relegate homosexuals to the separate and unequal status of civil unions.

Bob Dole and President Bush, respectively, saw to it that a public display like Buchanan's did not reoccur at the 1996 and 2000 conventions, but the president has shown clearly where his heart is by at every turn supporting the positions of the Religious Right and implementing them wherever possible through regulation or legislation.

In his blistering dissent in *Lawrence v. Texas*, Supreme Court Justice Scalia castigated the majority for having "taken sides in the culture wars" (as if he hadn't!) and "adopted the homosexual agenda."

Just what is this infamous "homosexual agenda"? It is simply to be treated with respect and equality. It is to pursue their lives like everyone else . . . to be free from discrimination in the workplace, to be protected legally from vicious, hate-based violence, to be able to enter into committed, loving relationships with the same legal rights and responsibilities as heterosexual couples, to raise their children in supportive, loving homes (gays and lesbians do have children, both natural and adopted, and studies have consistently shown that these children are as psychologically healthy as children of heterosexual couples[38]), and to have a zone of privacy in their bedrooms which is free from government intrusion. It is to be free from intolerance. It is to have the right to "life, liberty, and the pursuit of happiness." *Lawrence v. Texas* has righted a major past wrong of this society, but erasing the embedded discrimination in so many areas of the lives of gays and lesbians will take more action and more time.

Republicans/Conservatives and the Religious Right have placed the epithet of "antifamily" on Democrats/Liberals for their support of a woman's right to choose and for their support of gay rights. Yet in what way are these positions antifamily or destructive of the family? In fact, they are not. If any- thing, both these policies strengthen the family . . . in the one instance by not bringing unwanted and unloved children into this world, creating a danger for both the child, the family and society, and in the other by encouraging more families to be accepting of their gay and lesbian children and ending the cruel and painful separation that in the past was the norm.

Moreover, the term "family" encompasses much more to-day than the traditional two-parent, male/female nucleus with children. Many couples have no children and have no inten- tion to have children; many households with children have only a single parent; many committed, loving relationships are same-sex, both with and without children, natural and adopted . . . but all these social units are families. All of these have a valuable role to play in providing stability to our society. By supporting same-sex civil marriage, Democrats/Liberals would in no way threaten heterosexual marriage but rather seek to expand the positive benefits to society of civil marriage by making it available to all, gay and straight, equally.

Ironically, Republican/Conservative policies that don't support universal health insurance or give short shrift to the economics of the working-class poor are far more harmful to a family and thus "antifamily" than the Democrat/Liberal positions on choice and gay rights.

Similarly, the proposed constitutional amendment ban- ning same-sex civil marriages, supported by President Bush and the Religious Right, would pervert our Constitution, long the source of our liberty, equality, and individual rights, into a document which codifies discrimination against a minority for the first time since the slaves were freed and women were given the vote. It is they who threaten the foundations of our Republic, not the Democrats.

Democrats/Liberals must rally the populace on these various gay and lesbian rights issues by going back again to the nation's roots. They must present them as issues of fairness and justice, of the right of *all* citizens to "life, liberty and the pursuit of happiness." Given that homosexuality is not a result of individual choice, but rather a combination of genetics and environment, there is no longer any valid public policy reason to discriminate against gays and lesbians. Indeed, to do so would be immoral, because it would be punishing them for their "status," something over which they have no control.

The Republicans/Conservatives must be shown to be out of step with the majority and isolated; the Religious Right must not be allowed to impose its tenets on the majority of mainstream Americans. The fire of the right must be fought with the fire of reason from the liberals.

CHAPTER 7
Security

The only thing we have to fear is fear itself.
　　—Franklin D. Roosevelt, Inaugural Address, March 4, 1933

THE SECURITY AND PRIVACY of the individual is another concept central to the Constitution. Freedom from government intrusion is guaranteed by the Fourth Amendment, which protects each person from unreasonable search and seizure, and the Fifth Amendment, which provides protection from forced confessions. But security in another sense is also very important in that part of the government's role in securing our rights to life, liberty, and the pursuit of happiness lies in its police and national-defense functions. We all need the security of being free from criminal assaults, and more recently, terrorist assaults.

Here again, the framers of the Constitution achieved an equitable balance between these two potentially conflicting goals, with, however, the right of the individual to be free from unreasonable government intrusion and coercion being predominant. These rights have falsely been labeled by Conservatives and much of the press as technicalities that prevent the police from doing their jobs and allow criminals to escape punishment. To a large extent, the public has bought that perspective because it does not see itself as being protected by these rights. After all, they are not criminals. They do not under- stand that these rights protect them, the innocent, from over- reaching law-enforcement officers. They do not understand what life would be like if those rights did not exist.

Yet we have just engaged in a war to overthrow a despot whose tyrannical regime of fear was possible because such rights did not exist in Iraq. Indeed, such rights do not exist in any totalitarian/fascist state. The public needs to be vividly shown how we all benefit from the rights given to the accused.

Over the past few years, there has been more and more evidence through the use of DNA testing of both the intentional fabrication of cases and negligent bungling of cases by our police and prosecution systems, resulting in many inno- cent men and women being brought to trial and convicted, some even being sentenced to death. Innocent lives have been destroyed. There is no way of knowing how many people currently in custody were the victims of such actions. Governor Ryan of Illinois considered the situation to be so fraught with potential injustice that in January 2003 he commuted the death sentences of all 156 inmates on death row.

This abuse has not just happened in one city but in cities all around the country. For example, on August 2, 2003, the *New York Times* reported that "the U.S. Attorney in Detroit is reviewing what could exceed more than 100 criminal cases to see whether any convictions should be overturned as a result of the indictment of 17 Detroit police officers on corruption charges [including] conducting illegal searches, making unlawful arrests, using excessive force, falsifying police reports, and planting evidence."

There is also ample evidence that police brutality is not uncommon. Many cases in various cities have received media publicity, but many cases undoubtedly remain hidden. As reported in the *Chicago Reader,* during a twenty-year period from 1973–1991, suspects were subjected to "savage torture" by detectives and police in one area of Chicago, quoting a former city attorney. Complaints included electric shock, suf- focation, burnings, attacks on the genitals, severe beating, and mock executions. A former city detective complained of the gang-crimes unit activity in a particular case, "Their idea is you go out and pick up two thousand pounds of nigger and eventually you'll get the right one."[39]

The public must be made aware that those lives could have been our brothers, our sisters, our neighbors, ourselves. At the same time, a strong and well-functioning professional police force and law-enforcement agency—adequately staffed, well-trained, and disciplined—is critical to the maintenance of a democratic society. Democrats/Liberals should strongly support these agencies, not by blindly standing behind them as the Republicans/Conservatives do, but by insuring that they receive proper training and supervision and adequate funding so that they enforce the law as it is meant to be enforced under our Constitution, with respect for every individual and his or her rights.

The tendency of the Republicans/Conservatives to side with police power over the rights of individuals has taken a new twist and received a new authority since 9/11. The Bush administration has sought in numerous ways to curtail rights against government intrusion guaranteed by the Constitution under the guise that we are in a war for our survival. The Bush administration cleverly manipulated public reaction by packaging many of these restrictions as part of "The Patriot Act." The public, primarily concerned with security and worried about additional terrorist attacks, approves a "strong" government and seems to willingly go along with these tactics because they've been told they are the necessary cost of a strong homeland security plan. Yet most reports agree that, except for improved airport security, we are hardly more secure now than we were on 9/11.

Most recently, on September 10, 2003, the Bush administration announced plans to erode our constitutional rights even further. Federal agents would be allowed to issue subpoenas to demand private records and compel testimony without the approval of a judge or even a federal prosecutor. Generally, release on bail in terrorism investigations would be prohibited. Even Senator Arlen Spector (R-PA) said he is troubled by elements of Bush's plan "because I'm concerned that it may be too sweeping.   The Justice Department has gone too far."[40]

In response to criticism of these plans, a Justice Department spokesman made this statement, "It's our responsibility when we find weaknesses in the law to make suggestions to Congress to fix them   We don't want to tie the hands of prosecutors behind their backs."[41] This statement is shocking in that it seems to disregard the fact that we have a Constitu- tion that sets certain standards by which all laws and actions by government must abide. The rights set forth in these standards are central to what makes ours a free society and separates us from totalitarian regimes.

What is the philosophical difference between a terrorist investigation and an investigation into a serial killer, a serial rapist, a major drug ring, or any serious crime of violence? Where does one draw the line once you allow our constitutional protections to be ignored? This is a road fraught with grave dangers for our country, for each and every one of us, because it challenges the most basic elements of American liberty and our freedom from unreasonable government intrusion, elements that have stood the test of time and have served us well.

Americans are still grieving and recovering from the terrifying events of 9/11. That such a strong, coordinated attack by foreign insurgents could take place on our soil was a severe shock to the nation's feeling of insular security and left people feeling vulnerable. Time will be needed to heal these wounds and adjust to the new reality. But is this the basis for the pervasive fear that still seems to grip so many Americans at some level of their psyche two years after 9/11?

Risk is a factual part of the life of every American. Americans, without meaning to sound callous, die or are seriously injured on a daily basis from a variety of causes. On an actuarial basis, the probabilities of being involved in a terrorist attack are quite remote compared to other possible causes of death or maiming. For example, while horrific, we do not live in constant fear of being in a serious car accident, and we certainly don't stop driving. Even when we've been involved in an accident, it doesn't impact how we proceed with our lives, except that perhaps we are a bit more careful.

I submit that the reason for this continuing feeling of insecurity and pervasive fear lies primarily in the actions of the Bush administration. Why do we have publicized color-coded terror risk warnings issued by the Department of Homeland Security which have no impact other than creating fear in the mind of the public? Why have Attorney General Ashcroft and other members of the administration continued to beat the drum of danger in our midst? Why hasn't President Bush calmed the public by putting the risk of terrorism in perspec- tive, rather than continuing his saber rattling. Why didn't President Bush quote FDR's famous and true Great Depres- sion statement, "The only thing we have to fear is fear itself"?

Critics of the Bush administration suggest everything from pure political calculation (the security issue is Bush's strongest card with the American people) to giving them an excuse to increase military spending (defense industry corporations are major Republican donors) and restrict Fourth and Fifth Amendment rights (a favored conservative issue). I would not hazard a guess as to what their motivation is. But we know that the various measures taken by the Bush administration in the name of fear have for the most part had no measurable impact on our actual security. They have, however, accomplished the three objectives mentioned.

Certainly, measures need to be taken by the government to increase our security. But there is a limit to what the government or individuals can or should do, unless we want to live in a guarded police state. We live in a country with vast, remote and therefore porous borders. We know from our experience in trying to stop the flow of illegal immigrants from Mexico that the answer lies not in securing our boarders, but in help- ing improve living conditions and opportunities in Mexico.

Democrats/Liberals must stand up against this exploitation and propagation of fear. They must put the terrorist threat in perspective for the American people. And they must argue for a foreign policy, as discussed in chapters 10 and 11, that works towards building strong indigenous economies in the developing world and supports their legitimate political aspirations. The answer to terrorism does not lie in restricting our individ- ual constitutional rights.

In Robert Bolt's *A Man for All Seasons,* Thomas More's son-in-law says that he would cut down every law in England to get the devil, and More responds, "And when the last law was down, and the Devil turned on you, where would you hide? . . . This country's planted thick with laws from coast to coast . . . if you cut them down . . . d'you really think you could stand upright in the winds that would blow then? Yes, I'd give the Devil the benefit of the law for my own safety's sake."

The Democrats/Liberals must make the public understand that these repressive actions are decidedly against the American way, that they are unnecessary, and that these tactics do not just threaten the rights of accused terrorists and criminals; they threaten the rights and the freedom of us all.

CHAPTER 8
The Environment and Energy Policy

As crude a weapon as a cave man's club, the chemical barrage has been hurled against the fabric of life.

—Rachel Carson, *Silent Spring*

The fundamental principles of ecology govern our lives wherever we live, and . . . we must wake up to this fact or be lost.

—Karin Sheldon, *Ms.*, September 1973

I believe each individual is naturally entitled to do as he pleases . . ., so far as it in no wise interferes with any other man's rights.

—Abraham Lincoln, Speech, July 10, 1858

THE ISSUE OF ENVIRONMENTAL PROTECTION comes down to a very basic question: to what extent do the owners of property have the right to be free from government regulation that protects the public at large and is in the public good? And a re-lated question: to what extent are government lands available for private industrial exploitation rather than being preserved as wilderness for the greater public good?

Here again the question is how to balance the right of the individual (in this case a business) to be free from government intrusion with the duty of the government to secure the right of the broader society to life, liberty, and the pursuit of happi-ness by protecting the environment.

The Bush administration, not surprisingly, supports the industrialists in their desire to be free of as much government interference in their industries as possible, and to open up as much federal land for their use as possible. During the two and one-half years of this administration, hardly a week has passed without some effort, either at the regulatory or legislative level, to weaken environmental protections in favor of oil, coal, logging, mining, chemical, power, and other industrial interests.

Here are but a few examples. For a complete list go to www.nrdc.org/bushrecord.

- The Environmental Protection Agency has proposed changes to the Clean Air Act that would provide the nation's oldest and dirtiest power plants and refineries with loopholes exempting them from installing modern pollution controls when they upgrade or expand their facilities in ways that increase emissions.[42]
- The EPA and Army Corps of Engineers have proposed policies to relax and, in some cases, end Clean Water Act protection for millions of acres of wetlands and other waterways; eliminate corporate liability for "factory farm" pollution; and exempt mining waste from regulation as a pollutant under federal law.[43]
- The Forest Service and other federal agencies propose to eliminate requirements for environmental review and public participation when considering logging, mining, drilling, development and other projects in all 155 national forests and on millions of acres of public lands.[44]
- After a federal judge ruled that the Department of Energy acted illegally when it attempted to abandon millions of gallons of highly radioactive waste in underground storage tanks at three nuclear weapons facilities by reclassifying it as "incidental" waste, the agency asked Congress to overturn the court decision.[45]
- Bush's "Clear Skies" Bill, if passed, would actually allow more pollution than is allowed under current leg-

islation. Polluters could exceed established caps by buying unused pollution allowances from other energy producers.[46] So rather than being an effort, as trumpeted by Bush, to provide our children with cleaner air, it is a concession to Bush's industrial backers by lessening controls.

- Bush's "Healthy Forest" Bill is again a prescription for anything but that. Using as a pretense the desire to control destructive forest fires through thinning, the bill would instead allow significant logging of large and medium mature trees and the building of logging roads into remote areas with greatly reduced public re- view. Research has shown that the way to reduce forest fires is to thin the forest floor by removing dense undergrowth which acts as tinder, not by removing mature trees. This is especially important in forests near communities. But loggers are primarily interested in the mature trees, not in cleaning up the forest.[47] Both these bills are examples of the use of misleading manipulative packaging in an attempt to fool the public

The Clinton administration, other Democratic/Liberal administrations, and Democrat-controlled congresses by contrast have moved to protect the environment, and thus either directly or indirectly the public, by limiting the freedom of industry to pollute and degrade the environment through regulation. This was not regulation for regulation's sake. There are critical health and other quality of life issues that are at stake here.

History has shown that industry cannot be trusted to monitor, regulate, and police itself. The efforts by Bush and the Republicans to limit regulatory controls and to instead rely on voluntary measures are disingenuous. There have been too many instances of corporate social irresponsibility over the years and certainly most recently. It is the nature of the beast that corporations will try to get away with whatever they can in order to hold their costs down and increase their profits, re- gardless of the impact of their operations on the health and well-being of the broader society.

Democrats/Liberals must make the public aware of this continual assault on their health and the environment by the Bush administration and Republicans/Conservatives in Con- gress. The media have not done a good job of bringing these matters to the attention of the general public, and so it is most- ly unaware of what has been happening.

If industry complains that the cost of more restrictive regu- lation would be too costly for them, they must be reminded of EPA research that shows that the societal costs of ongoing pol- lution are far greater than the direct costs to industry.[48] While the cost of complying with such regulation would certainly cut into profits, the regulations are economically sound in that these industries would remain profitable. They must be re- minded that they function within a broader framework of so- ciety, which places certain obligations and restraints on busi- nesses in the interest of the general welfare. They are after all there to provide a service to the public as well as make money.

But the issue of the environment goes beyond our imme- diate or even long-term health and enjoyment of the natural environment. The government's energy policy is an environ- mental issue that threatens the future well-being of our econ- omy and our national security.

Ever since the Arab oil embargo of 1973–74, the country has been well aware of the danger that lies in our dependence on foreign oil for much of our energy needs. But beyond that danger, our dependence generally on fossil fuels such as oil and gas for energy are long-term disasters waiting to happen because fossil fuels are a nonrenewable source of energy. They are the product of millions of years of geologic activity. Once they are gone, they are gone.

In light of these facts, there are only two ways to in the long term provide energy security for the United States: a combination of conservation/reduced consumption of energy and the creation of alternative energy sources.

Both those efforts were a high priority for President Jimmy Carter during his term of office. Partly through regulation and executive order, and partly through his own example of lowering the thermostat in the White House in winter and raising it in the summer, President Carter managed to accomplish the seemingly impossible task of getting Americans to use less energy. The result was a cut in our importation of foreign oil from 8.6 billion barrels a day at the beginning of his term to almost 4.3 billion barrels a day in 1982, a year after he left office.[49]

He was less successful at his efforts to encourage the development of alternative energy sources because big corporate energy interests opposed these initiatives. And so, not surprisingly, the politicians in Congress who receive large campaign contributions from these interests did not support his efforts.

During the Reagan administration, and all subsequent administrations, all efforts to reduce consumption were abandoned. Alternative energy development has received barely token support. As a result, our dependence on foreign oil is higher now than it ever was—10.4 billions barrels a day in 2002. And Bush's proposed FY 2004 budget slashes what meager support there has been by cutting spending on zero- energy buildings by 50 percent, biomass by 19 percent, and wind research by 5.5 percent.[50]

Once again, using a problem as a pretext, the current Bush administration has developed an energy policy that has basically only one element—the opening up of more domestic oil fields for exploration, whether they be in the Arctic National Wildlife Refuge, in other federal wilderness areas, or offshore. This policy has only one beneficiary—the big energy interests. It will not benefit the average American even in the short term (for example, despite more natural gas wells being drilled in the first years of the Bush administration than in any compa- rable period, natural gas production has remained flat and supplies are considerably lower[51]), and certainly not in the long term, because these efforts, if successful, would just deplete our finite energy resources all the more quickly, in addition to their other negative environmental impacts.

Indeed, even the manner in which the Bush administration developed its energy policy shows how contrary to the American social contract it is. Remember Lincoln's words, "government of the people, by the people, and for the people." In developing its energy policy, a task force headed by Vice President Cheney (himself a former oil man, as is President Bush) held a series of closed meetings at which only industry interests were invited to speak. No contrary voices representing the broader public interest were invited. The administration has been sued to reveal information about this process, but the administration has yet to release the list of people whom the Cheney task force met with in secrecy. The motto of this administration is clearly "government of industry, by industry, and for industry."

Yes, Bush and Congress are supporting research in one alternative energy technology—hydrogen-powered automobiles. Perhaps because of the pressure caused by the development of this technology in Japan and Europe, a sustained research effort in this area may actually occur.

Another way of conserving energy would be to build high-speed regional rail systems to divert traffic from high-energy-consuming cars and planes to trains. Other countries make very good use of modern trains to speed passengers efficiently to regional destinations of up to five hundred miles. The fed- eral government, however, is still stuck in the "what's good for General Motors is good for the country" mentality. Trains are viewed as potential competitors to the automobile and plane industries and have no counterweight to those strong lobbies. As a result, Congress maintains that railroads should be self-sustaining and should not receive federal subsidies. Amtrak is faced with this mantra every year.

Yet isn't the federally funded highway system an enormous subsidy for the automobile industry? The highway system has cost the federal government $1.2 trillion from 1958 to 1991. Some of this money came from user taxes and license fees, but the net cost to the federal government of this automobile sub-sidy still is estimated to be between $111 billion a year[52] and $41 billion a year.[53]

Government investment in building high-speed railroad tracks and infrastructure would be the practical equivalent of its spending on highway construction, but at far less cost. The estimate is that the capital costs for fully developed, federally designated high-speed rail corridors, including the northeast corridor, would be between $50 and $70 billion over twenty years.[54] That is less than two years' federal subsidy for the highway system. But, the High-Speed Rail Investment Act continues to languish in Congress.

Democrats/Liberals must take the issue of energy policy and control by industrial interests to the American people. This is not being antibusiness; it is a matter of forcing business to be responsible not just to their stockholders but to the larger public and society by conducting their operations with due regard for its health and well-being. It is about government being supportive of business development and business needs but not being subservient to them. It is about placing a limit on corporate greed. It is about meeting the public need to les- sen our dependence on foreign oil and fossil fuels in general.

CHAPTER 9
Taxes and the Economy

My fellow Americans, ask not what your country can do for you—ask what you can do for your country.
      —John F. Kennedy, Inaugural Address, January 20, 1961

THE GOVERNMENT, through its various monetary policies and spending, has a major impact on the health of the country's economy and thus the job market, as well as many of the other issues that are discussed in this book. This is another mechanism through which it fulfills its role of securing for all citizens the right to "life , liberty, and the pursuit of happiness." Tax policies, in turn, are a critical part of that mechanism.

Taxes are an expression of government power over the individual in recognition of the individual's obligation to contribute to the maintenance and welfare of the government and society. As such, the issue of taxes must again be discussed with reference to the context provided by the Declaration and the American social contract, for the issue revolves once more around the balance between private rights and broader societal interests and the role of government.

Until the ratification in 1913 of the Sixteenth Amend- ment, which authorized the federal income tax, taxes that were levied by the federal, state, and local governments were primar- ily property taxes, sales or use taxes (taxes on goods bought in or out of state respectively), as well as "head" taxes (taxes levied on a per person basis, such as a poll tax). Use, sales, and head taxes are by their very nature "regressive," which is to say that the burden of taxes falls disproportionately on those of lower income; they pay a higher percentage of their income in such taxes than do those with more income.

For example, take two individuals, one of whom has an income of $20,000 a year and the other an income of $100,000, who purchase the same quantity of cigarettes, clothing, groceries, and other common items, and say that the yearly sales taxes paid on those items is $1,000. While that $1,000 represents the same tax rate for both on the cost of goods bought, the lower-income person has paid 5 percent of his income in sales taxes, while the higher-income person has paid only 1 percent.

The enactment of the federal income tax brought with it the concept of using the tax system to redistribute wealth. It is a "progressive" tax system in that the more income one has, the higher the rate of taxation. The principle behind this progressive tax system lies at the heart of the American social contract, with its balance between rights of the individual and the interests of the broader society, which result in obligations of the individual. Thus, those with greater wealth pay more to the government to support its work and its efforts to level the playing field, to provide those born in less fortunate circumstances the education and health opportunities that are critical to making the "right to life, liberty, and the pursuit of happiness" a real right. It is also a reflection of the reality that those with less money need every dollar they earn to meet their immediate needs; they have no discretionary income to speak of.

There are various ways, however, in which the progressive system of taxation expounded by our government is not honored in actual practice. First, the tax code is filled with loopholes, which allow those with money to escape paying their share of taxes. These loopholes result from the pressure on congressmen (both Republicans and Democrats, though more money goes to the Republicans) by a large variety of interest groups. The bottom line is that those with higher incomes pay a far lower rate of taxes than the tax table would indicate, and the system is thus far less progressive than it appears.

Second, Republicans constantly push for a reduction in taxes on the wealthy and corporations, claiming that it is good for the economy and that those with lower incomes will benefit as a result. This "trickle down" theory was at the core of what has come to be known as Reaganomics, or supply-side economic theory, and it was proven to be a fiasco. The Reagan experience showed that there was no trickle down, the rich prospered while the poor stagnated,[55] government deficits zoomed ever higher, and ultimately taxes had to be increased.

Our government was not created to protect the interests of the rich and big business. It was created to protect the interests of *all* the people. The motto, "What's good for General Motors is good for the country," has long since been discredited. Certainly, Democrats/Liberals understand that a strong business community is vital to a strong economy, and government policies need to encourage and support business growth. But just because a policy is good for big business does not mean that it automatically is good for the economy and the broader society; indeed it could be and in many cases has been actually harmful.

The Bush administration has pushed through major tax cuts quite similar to those of the Reagan years, causing as they did previously a huge increase in the federal deficit (once again to record levels) and cutbacks in federal aid to the states, creat- ing in turn record deficit problems for states and cities which have put some on the verge of bankruptcy. This is causing states and cities to either raise taxes or cut back on services. And, as will be seen in the following pages, the problem is only going to get worse over the next few years.

Third, when all taxes are considered, not just the income tax, but state and local sales and excise taxes, social security tax, and Medicare tax, our tax system is far less progressive. In the early 1990s, to combat budget shortfalls caused by the recession, states typically increased sales and excise taxes, which are regressive. When a stronger economy allowed taxes to be cut, the cut was given through the income tax, which disproportionately went to higher income families, not through repealing the regressive tax increases. This has made the combined sys- tem more regressive.[56]

Likewise, Bush's recent tax cuts have made the federal income tax more regressive for the same reason—that is, the rich will disproportionately benefit from the tax cut. But here again, Bush has misled the public. In announcing the tax cut package, he stated, "These tax reductions will bring real and immediate benefits to middle-income Americans. Ninety-two million Americans will keep an average of $1,083 more of their own money." But the use of the arithmetic "average" for all taxpayers is misleading because the package was tilted heavily towards the wealthy. According to the Urban-Brookings Tax Policy Center, households in the middle quintile (in other words, middle-income Americans) will receive an average tax cut of only $217.[57]

Fairness to the working poor and middle-class families whose dollars must go to meeting immediate needs of housing, food, transportation, and their children's education requires that a way be found to make federal and state income taxes more progressive and perhaps alter the mix of taxes so that fed- eral, state, and local governments receive the revenues they need to accomplish their tasks while reducing the burden on the poor and middle class.

No one likes paying taxes, but they are necessary. And, consistent with the American social contract, those with great- er means have a greater obligation to support the government's work and its role in leveling the playing field and providing equal opportunities for those less fortunate. That is the price of living in our society. Democrats/Liberals must make this point strongly. Fairness demands it. In so doing they can certainly point out that our rate of taxation, even according to the tax table, is far less than *any* other industrialized country.

In addition to the Bush administration's tax policies being regressive, their impact on the economy has been an unmitigated disaster.

- We have gone from having a surplus of $236.4 billion in 2000,[58] the last year of the Clinton administration, to record deficits of $375 billion for 2003 and a pro-jected deficit of $477 billion for 2004 under Bush (al-though as a percentage of Gross National Product, the deficits of the Reagan years were even higher).[59]
- The unemployment rate has soared from a near record post-WWII peacetime low of 4 percent when Clinton left office to an average of 6 percent for all of 2003.[60] In practical terms, that means that 2.3 million jobs have been lost since President Bush took office, includ-ing almost 800,000 since the economic recovery offi-cially started in November 2001. Despite small gains in the latter part of 2003, this remains a jobless recov-ery.[61]

Besides having a major impact on state and local government, the overall economy, and the American worker, the last round of Bush's tax cuts, enacted on the eve of the war in Iraq, also resulted in cuts to needed and popular government programs. For example:

- The FY 2004 budget as passed by the House on a par-ty-line vote cut $14.6 billion in veterans programs, including money for disabilities caused by war wounds, rehabilitation and health care, pensions for low- income veterans, education and housing benefits, and even burial benefits. "Well-to-do" veterans, defined as earning $26,000, would now be charged premiums for medical care.[62]

- In 2002, the "No Child Left Behind" Act was a signature piece of President Bush's claim to being strong on education. The Bush budget for FY 2004 cut funding for the act by one-third, from the authorized $18.5 billion down to $12.3 billion.[63]

Republicans/Conservatives are fond of calling Democrats/Liberals the "tax and spend" party, with the implication that Democratic/Liberal spending is irresponsible. But actually, quite the contrary has been true. When Democrats/Liberals seek to spend large amounts of money, it is to address pressing national issues that need attention, thus fulfilling the government's constitutional role. The issue may be a social one such as health insurance, it may be an economic one such as the need to jumpstart an ailing economy through government spending, or it may be an issue of military defense. But what- ever the reason, it has in general been a sound one and an ap- propriate one.

Ironically, as the chart on the next page, based on data from the Congressional Budget Office,[64] shows, it has actually been the Democrats who in the last two administrations have been fiscally conservative and responsible, seeking to reduce deficits and balance the budget, while the three Republican administrations have been fiscally irresponsible. While the Republicans have consistently cut taxes (mainly for the imme- diate benefit of corporations, who lobby heavily for reduced taxes, and rich individuals), they have not cut spending. They

BUDGET DEFICITS/SURPLUSES
OF RECENT ADMINISTRATIONS,
LAST YEAR AND TERM
(in billions of dollars)
from Congressional Budget Office figures

President	Last Year In Office	Deficit/Surplus In Last Year	Total Deficit During Term
Carter	1980	(73.9)[1]	(227.4)
Reagan	1988	(155.2)	(1,338.6)
G.H.W. Bush	1992	(290.4)	(933.4)
Clinton	2000	236.4[2]	(320.6)
G.W. Bush	2004	(477)[3]	(882.5)[4]

1. For the first three years of his term, Carter reduced the deficit to 53, 59, and 40 billion respectively, but the deficit increased in his last year as a result of the Arab oil embargo.

2. Under Clinton, there was first a steady decrease in the deficit followed by an increase in the surplus.

3. Under Bush, there was a drop in the surplus during his first year, followed by two years of increasing deficits, with the CBO projecting another record deficit for 2004, contrary to projections at the start of his term which showed major surpluses extending on for a number of years.

4. This figure includes projected figures through the end of Bush's term. Note: These actual and projected deficits are only partially caused by 9/11, the war in Afghanistan, and the war in Iraq. A major factor is re- duced revenue as a result of the tax cuts.

could indeed be called the "cut taxes and spend" party. Theirs is a very unsound approach as has been shown by the actual results.

And, to make matters worse, Republicans/Conservatives tend to spend taxpayer dollars differently. Rather than spending it to help alleviate the social and economic conditions that limit opportunities for many Americans, they favor requests for corporate subsidies and hugely expensive military toys that often fail to live up to their promise and certainly do not increase our national security to an extent that would justify the price. They are also not opposed to the time-honored congressional practice of "pork barrel" projects (as indeed most Democrats admittedly are not)—projects that have no purpose other than to provide a benefit to the voters back home as a way of staying in office.

Democrats/Liberals must present the real facts clearly to the American voter and claim as their justifiable mantle the party of fiscal responsibility and a strong economy.

And, if we are to have a deficit, let it be one which has the goal of directly improving the lives of our middle-class citizens, the American worker, and the poor, rather than primarily benefiting the rich and corporations. Let it be a deficit that has a long-term beneficial impact on our economy through a combination of targeted spending and tax policies that sustain a diverse local economy, strengthen the consumer base, and encourage businesses to invest in capital improvements.

CHAPTER 10
The American Worker and the Global Economy

I feel betrayed. I keep hearing about the jobs being created, but I don't see them.
> —Billy Johnson, programmer and lifelong Republican,
> *Time*, March 1, 2004

The sky is the limit here.
> —Dharin Shah, 26-year-old engineer, India,
> *Newsweek*, February 3, 2003

The triumph of capitalism only in the West could be a recipe for economic and political disaster.
> —Hernando de Soto, *The Mystery of Capital*

As IMPORTANT AS A FAIR TAX SYSTEM is to maintaining the American social contract and fiscal responsibility is to a strong long-term economy, the impact of other government policies on the job market is perhaps even more critical, both to securing the right of all citizens to life, liberty, and the pursuit of happiness and to maintaining a strong economy.

The American worker is the backbone of the American economy. Whether blue collar or white collar, whether skilled or unskilled, whether managing a major corporation or managing a local fast-food operation . . . each individual American worker both contributes to and sustains the American economy. He or she contributes by producing a product or a service and sustains by consuming products and services. The continuing strength of a diverse local economy is a vital part of our country's economic health. Indeed, it is primarily the consumer, not big business, that has kept the economy afloat during the recent recession and recovery.

During the past few decades, various federal trade and financial policies combined with state and local business incentives in many areas of the country have encouraged the growth of high tech and service industry white collar companies while creating a very negative environment for blue collar industries. This has caused the loss of good-paying manufacturing jobs.[65]

This is bad public policy. Even in our "post-industrial" era, manufacturing remains crucial to a diverse economy and thus to our prosperity. Given that more than 60 percent of U.S. workers lack college degrees, and that manufacturing jobs for such workers pay roughly 20 percent more than other sectors, the loss of manufacturing jobs contributes to a loss of earnings and consumer power that is bad for our economy and contributes to the increasing income inequality.[66] Democrats/Liberals must argue for an industrial policy that encourages a broad spectrum of jobs including blue collar manufacturing.

In addition to the government policies and other factors that have traditionally impacted jobs in the United States, the past two decades have seen the emergence of a new factor—the global economy. Free-trade policies and more recently the internet and the development of high-speed data networks are having a major effect, though no one really knows with a comfortable degree of certainty the scope of what that impact is or will be.

This much is clear, however. The law of comparative advantage is operating to shift an increasing number of jobs, including more lately high-skill jobs, to developing countries. Initially, free trade resulted in the exodus of jobs in certain manufacturing sectors, such as clothing, shoes, and cheap electronics, because of the cheap labor available in Third World countries. NAFTA expanded the range of manufacturing jobs that were lost. In theory, the jobs lost would be more than off-set by an increase in jobs resulting from an increase in U.S. exports flowing from free trade. Whether that has happened or not is a matter of dispute even in the more controlled environment of NAFTA.

With the development of advanced communications systems, the internet, and high-speed data networks came the ability for companies to outsource simple, low-paying, repetitive white-collar jobs such as credit-card processing or writing software code.

Most recently, as reported in several magazines during 2003 including *Business Week*,[67] higher-level, well-paying jobs such as "drawing up detailed architectural blueprints, slicing and dicing a company's financial disclosures, or designing a revolutionary microprocessor" have been outsourced overseas to countries like India, China, and the Philippines where wages are lower and the supply of intelligent college graduates is plentiful. These countries are developing a trade advantage in new job fields that are far removed from the sweatshops that produce shoes and clothing.

What are the short- and long-term implications of this development for the American worker? One recent forecast says that three to four million high-wage jobs will be outsourced over the next ten years.[68] According to the *Business Week* ar- ticle, no one really knows because the rise of the global know- ledge industry is too new. It quotes Harvard University econ- omist Robert Z. Lawrence, a prominent free-trade advocate, "I still have faith that globalization will make us better off, but it's no more than faith."

While the number of jobs that may be lost are small relative to the total U.S. economy, and while millions of jobs are created and lost annually as part of the normal evolution of the economy, faith just isn't good enough when it comes to insuring the well-being of the American worker, on whom the strength of our economy depends every bit as much as the profitability of our businesses. If the net loss were to be a few million jobs, that would have the same impact on the American worker and the consumer economy as a recession, but on an ongoing basis.

As noted in a February 2004 New York Times article, however, many economists have more than faith.[69] They point to the events of the past several decades, and especially the more recent experience of high tech competition from low- wage economies, to say that the increase in productivity and reduced prices that have resulted from low cost production sources have resulted in a major expansion in industry in this country and the creation of new jobs here. They note that in the late 1990s, unemployment fell to 4% despite an aggressive expansion of outsourcing. The article also points out that the net loss of jobs we have seen during 2001-2003 has been caused by the recession, not the outsourcing of jobs. Another benefit noted as flowing from the abundance of these low-cost products is that they have helped keep our inflation rate low, which has allowed interest rates to remain low, which in turn encourages investment.

The economists quoted in the article acknowledge that this source of productivity growth, as with most sources, involves pain for many workers. But, the answer is not to cut off the source of productivity growth by returning to protectionism and ending free trade, just as it would be folly to return to the era of pre-automation, another major source of productivity increase and worker dislocation. That would clearly be bad for the overall economy and for workers as a whole.

Instead, Democrats/Liberals must challenge economists to develop models for this new global economy so that government policies can be developed to insure sufficient job growth and sufficient competitiveness in both higher-paying and lower-paying jobs to meet the needs of the American worker and to insure strong economic growth. To support job creation and competitiveness, we must also insure that our educational system provides the workforce with the training necessary to handle all levels of blue collar and white collar jobs in the 21st century work environment. And to help enable the American worker successfully make the difficult transition from the old to the new economy, the government must expand retraining programs and employment insurance.

Part of this economic policy review must, of necessity, deal with the development of Third World countries. In his book, *The Mystery of Capital*, the economist Hernando De Soto makes the statement, "The triumph of capitalism only in the West could be a recipe for economic and political disaster."[70] De Soto argues that if capitalism does not become indigenous in the Third World, if its benefits are seen as just residing in the elite few and multinational corporations, subversives feed- ing on class antagonisms and anticapitalist/anti-West resent- ment will destabilize those countries, foment revolution, and create anticapitalist governments. Indeed, that is part of the explanation for the huge resentment in the Islamic world that is fueling global terrorism and destabilizing those countries.

But I would put an additional spin on De Soto's state- ment. Because of the internet, the development of high-speed data networks, and the resulting rise of the global knowledge industry, an even greater crisis is facing the West if capitalism does not become indigenous in the Third World. That crisis arises from the competitive advantage in both skilled and non-skilled, in high-tech and low-tech jobs that will increasingly lie in the Third World because their standard of living and there- fore their salaries are so much lower than in the United States.

That advantage will lead to an ever-increasing loss of jobs in the U.S, with a resulting weakening of the domestic economy.

Much has been written about the short-term perspective of most modern CEOs and stockholders. Because of that perspective, the lure of accessing cheaper labor by outsourcing any job possible, and thus increasing profits, is irresistible. This is in keeping with the historical attitude of the capitalist West towards the Third World, which was seen as a venue to exploit and benefit from in whatever way possible, but without transferring the knowledge necessary for those countries to do it themselves.

When Japan underwent its major industrial and capital transformation in the 1950s and 1960s and started to become a force on the world economic scene, it was often criticized and belittled in the West at first for having "imitated" the West's ideas and products and later viewed with antagonism because of its success. Part of this attitude towards developing countries is a cultural/racial one. For example, when Germany rose out of the ashes of WWII, few voiced criticism of it or were antagonized by its industrial power because Germany was, after all, part of the West and a bulwark against Com- munism. Now Japan, because of its success, has been accepted as part of the West as well.

De Soto explains the failure of capitalism in the developing world in this way. It is one thing to give people in Third World countries jobs and thereby give the average person the ability to purchase watches and televisions and other consumer items. It is another to help countries create the procedural and structural building blocks that are necessary to create capital out of assets and that are accessible to the broader public, not just the elite few.

There has been no shortage of advice from the West on how to create open market economies, and both macro economic structures and property laws have been put in place. And some companies have been very good at transferring technology and control. But while such changes have opened up these countries to the West and allowed the local elite to prosper, these changes have not brought about capital transformation on any scale because the systems and laws were taken wholesale from the West. They do not reflect the realities and traditions of the local extralegal economy and are mired in administrative/bureaucratic obstacles.

In the new global information world, an enlightened self-interest requires that the short-sighted thinking of the past must come to an end. Any policies, whether governmental or private industrial, which make it more difficult for the Third World to develop and increase its standard of living must change. The U.S. government must do everything it can to support the development of indigenous capitalism. Such a pol- icy would have the attractive benefit of not only helping to lift the living standards of the people of the developing world, the- reby helping to secure their "Creator-endowed" right to life, liberty and the pursuit of happiness, but at the same time it would strengthen our economy and security, by creating a new competitive equilibrium. By helping others, we will help ourselves.

CHAPTER 11
Foreign Policy and Defense

In the councils of government, we must guard against the acquisition of unwarranted influence, whether sought or unsought, by the military-industrial complex. The potential for the disastrous rise of misplaced power exists and will persist.
—Dwight D. Eisenhower, Farewell Address, January 17, 1961

We yet realize that America's leadership and prestige depend, not merely upon our unmatched . . . strength, but on how we use our power in the interests of world peace and human betterment.   Any failure traceable to arrogance, or our lack of comprehension or readiness to sacrifice would inflict upon us grievous hurt both at home and abroad.
—Dwight D. Eisenhower, Farewell Address, January 17, 1961

THE PRIMARY ROLE of foreign policy is to protect the security of the United States. This has traditionally been done through a variety of means, such as establishing alliances to isolate enemies, having a strong military, encouraging the friendship of other nations through various aid programs, and extending our economic influence. Sometimes it has been effectuated through war, declared or otherwise, or clandestine operations to assassinate key opponents or topple governments.

American foreign policy has always been pragmatic, and indeed, it must be. At its core, however, our foreign policy should be consistent with the principles this country has always said it stands for—democracy, freedom, human rights, and the legitimate aspirations of all people as voiced in the Declaration of Independence.

Instead, U.S. foreign policy has been based primarily on the military and industrial interests of the United States—a very narrow definition of our national security interests. Even someone as conservative and military-oriented as President Eisenhower voiced his now prescient warning to beware the influence of the military-industrial complex on foreign policy.

As a result, foreign policy has often been taken to extremes, with the government resorting to gross stereotypes and a good-versus-evil analysis of who is friend or foe, an analysis that ultimately was often against the country's best interests. For example, during the cold war, the United States supported any government that was anti-Communist, regardless how ruthless the dictatorship, and tried to destabilize any Socialist, Communist-sympathetic country, regardless how democratic. The idea of wooing Socialist leaders as friends of the United States was an oxymoron to a succession of U.S. administrations.

A prime example was the support of the pro-West Mobuto regime in the Congo (who, over thirty years, ruthlessly exploited his own country) after the assassination of Socialist and Communist-friendly Patrice Lumumba, who had been elected president shortly after Congo's independence. Another prime example was the assassination of Salvador Allende and the toppling of his Socialist government in Chile. It was a harmful policy in that it bred anti-Americanism among the peoples of many countries.

American foreign policy has virtually never been based on what is in the best interests for the people of a country. It has been based primarily on the narrow military and industrial interests of the United States. The war in Vietnam had noth- ing to do with democracy for the Vietnamese; it was not about helping the Vietnamese people. It was purely a matter of combating Communism wherever it was found in order to protect the U.S.'s military and industrial interests.

After 9/11, the sole response of the Bush administration to the terrorist threat has been a military and police one with some public relations thrown in. Clearly military action was necessary and appropriate. But there has been no openness to the possibility that our long-term foreign policy in the region created an atmosphere in which the Islamic radicals could find willing recruits to their cause and be viewed as heroes and martyrs by the majority of the people in those countries. Yet, numerous experts have written articles about that very problem. This is an example of the lack of comprehension of which President Eisenhower warned. Certainly in today's world where terrorism is often not the direct product of a nation- state but rather a group of disaffected radicals who feed on broad public support, the administration's narrow view of for- eign policy is very dangerous.

For President Bush it was the familiar friend/foe analysis when he said, "You are either with us in the fight against terrorism, or you are an enemy of the United States." This gross simplification of world politics combined with his frequent references to God, while effective posturing at home, has again bred anti-Americanism, especially in Islamic countries. Despite the fact that it tried to distinguish this war from a war against Islam, Bush's strident posturing seemed to say something different to the Muslim world, and Osama bin Laden went from someone almost no one had heard of to become an overnight hero in the hearts and minds of the Muslim "street." The Muslim world was radicalized as never before.

Again, when the administration was preparing for war against Iraq, they ignored the argument that such a war would actually increase terrorism against the United States by further radicalizing the Arab populace, rather than decrease terrorism. They also ignored the assessment of many of our traditional allies and others that the war was not justified by the circumstances and proceeded without United Nations' approval. The war thus created a rupture with those allies and created substantial anti-American sentiment throughout Europe and the rest of the world. This Bush administration action is a perfect example of the arrogance of which President Eisenhower warned.

While no one would argue with the fact that Saddam Hussein was a tyrant and was a disaster for the people of Iraq, no serious person could truly believe that the United States made war against Iraq to free the Iraqi people. Indeed, that justification has only surfaced in administration statements after the war when no WMDs (weapons of mass destruction) were found, nor any links to al-Queda.

Which brings us to another very important policy question posed by the Iraq crisis and the Bush administration's policy of preemptive strikes; specifically, When is the United States justified in going to war without the support of the international community in the form of the United Nations? Clearly, the United States, as a sovereign country, has the right to protect itself from a clear and present danger, a significant threat to its security, whether it be from an actual attack or a planned attack, whether it be through forces of a foreign power or a state-backed terrorist organization. Democrats should be unequivocal on this policy issue.

When a country is attacked, the threat is clear and unambiguous. But, when a country has not been attacked, what level of danger and what level of proof of that danger should be required before Congress supports the president in going war, regardless whether the war is declared as such? It is in this area where the congressional Democrats, as a group, neglected their responsibilities in the run up to the war in Iraq.

First, at least as reported in the press, and even given Secretary Powell's later briefing of the U.N. Security Council, the level of danger posed by the claimed threat and the quality of proof of that threat was far below that necessary to meet a clear and present danger or a significant threat standard to justify unilaterally committing American troops to battle. Second, Congress, including most Democrats, gave President Bush a clear hand on whether to go to war or not based on his own assessment of the total situation as it developed. Given the weakness of the evidence and the claimed threat, at a minimum, the Democrats should have insisted on the president returning to Congress for a further resolution authorizing the commitment of troops to battle.

As an aside, another reason why it was argued that a war against Iraq was going to be counter-productive in our war against terrorism was that the war would require the shifting of important military resources away from the fight against al-Queda and Osama bin Laden in Afghanistan, and that indeed is what occurred. As reported by *Time,* a former Bush official has said that the reason why bin Laden and his operatives got away is "because we let up."[71]

Democrats/Liberals must argue that U.S. foreign policy should export or support democracy around the world regardless of whether the resulting government is pro- or anti-American. That policy must also show true concern and support for the legitimate economic needs and political aspirations of the people in Third World countries. The combined effect of these two approaches would likely be that many countries and their inhabitants that might at the start be anti-American would at the least become neutral, if not pro-American, thus greatly increasing our national security.

Here is one example of a current domestic policy that harms U.S. relations with developing countries and how that policy might be turned around. The United States paid its farmers roughly $16.4 billion in 2001 in agricultural subsidies[72] (the total figure for all the industrialized countries is $300 billion[73]). The result is that:

- Large corporate farmers in the United States get richer (71 percent of subsidies went to the 10 percent largest subsidized crop producers or 4 percent of all farmers; 60 percent of all farmers and ranchers do not collect any government subsidy payments because the crops and livestock they produce do not qualify for subsidy programs[74]).
- Commodity prices on the world market are depressed, undercutting the ability of developing countries to compete on the world market and thus improve their economies. Their share of global trade and investment has been collapsing as a result.[75]

What makes this illustration even more egregious is that the people of many of these countries, especially those in sub-Saharan Africa, face famine and starvation on a routine basis.

World Bank Chief Economist Nicholas Stern said recently, "It is hypocritical to preach the advantages of trade and markets and then erect obstacles in precisely those markets in which developing countries have a comparative advantage. That hypocrisy does not go unnoticed in developing countries. The recent Farm Bill in the United States and the recent agreement in Europe to delay the reform of the Common Agricultural Policy are deeply damaging."[76]

This is an example of the point made by De Soto that was quoted earlier in this manifesto, "The triumph of capitalism only in the West could be a recipe for economic and political disaster." It is in our enlightened self-interest from a security perspective to involve the broad base of people in Third World countries in the economic development and growth in those countries. In addition to the security self-interest, there are, as argued earlier, economic reasons to support the growth of indigenous capitalist economies in the Third World.

World Bank research has shown that cutting farm subsidies substantially would increase food production and resulting income substantially in developing countries. Of course, that involves a major dislocation at home and would be politically very difficult.

If one were going to think outside of the box, could one, with a single stroke, provide the desired income support to U.S. farmers, allow farmers in developing countries to compete effectively on the world market, and feed the world's starving masses? I suggest the following: rather than paying $16 billion in subsidies to U.S. farmers (or $300 billion worldwide), that money should be given as chits to developing countries that experience food shortages, with those chits being used to purchase foodstuffs from the donor countries. In this way, U.S. farmers would still get their money, world commodity prices would not be depressed so farmers in developing countries can compete and help their economies, and the people in these countries would have food to eat. It would be a much more productive use of the same tax dollars.

Such actions, together with a strong military and a strong democracy at home, would increase the credibility of the United States and the respect with which the United States is held around the world. That combination of factors is what is needed to increase America's security.

Republicans/Conservatives have for decades saddled the Democrats with the label of being "soft on defense" and "soft on Communism." Yet what is the evidence? Democratic presidents have led us in World War II, the Korean War, and the Vietnam War. Democrat presidents and Democratic- controlled Congresses have steadfastly supported funding for a strong military. Where they differ from the Republicans/Conservatives is that they look closely at what the military requests, pruning out at least some worthless military projects, rather than giving them almost a blank check as the Republicans/Conservatives do. Democrats/Liberals have consistently fought for responsible use of taxpayer dollars.

Yes, the 1972 Democratic presidential campaign of George McGovern and the primary campaign of Eugene McCarthy were both antiwar. But in the context of the Vietnam War, the positions of both men were strong and courageous. The defense establishment, the CIA, and the military/industrial complex had led the United States into a blind alley, an ill- conceived war with no acceptable exit or victory strategy, which resulted in the deaths of fifty-eight thousand, mostly young, American boys. It had resulted in the dislocation of the American economy. It had made the United States, long a bea- con of freedom for the world, a pariah and bully to much of the world. It was a policy disaster in every sense. It was without doubt a wrong war, a war which even many of its strongest supporters later concluded should never have happened and was against our best interests.

And what about being soft on Communism? Two wars were fought to stem the tide of Communism—the Korean War and the Vietnam War, both of which were entered into by Democratic presidents. The only way in which the Democrats/Liberals have historically been soft on Communism is that they fought the outrages and lies of Senator McCarthy's (R-WI) House Committee on Un-American Activities in the early 1950s. They sought to defend the right of Americans to free speech and free association guaranteed by the First Amendment, and to protect lives from being destroyed based on an out-of-control witch hunt. McCarthy was of course discredited after only several years in the limelight and disappeared from public life, but Richard Nixon, who gained his initial public fame working with McCarthy on the committee, went on to greater prominence, and ultimately, greater ignominy.

Democrats/Liberals must knock down this perennial Republican straw dog of being soft on defense. They must remind voters of the true historical facts about Democratic presidents and congresses. They must argue that blind support of military budget requests makes one fiscally irresponsible, not strong on defense.

EPILOGUE

WE, AS A NATION, stand at a crossroad. There is a strong movement afoot to replace the historically fundamentally liberal policies of our government, which are rooted in the Declaration of Independence and the Constitution, with policies informed more by the radical conservatism of the neo-conservatives and the Religious Right.

- It is a movement to restrict personal freedoms while increasing business/industrial freedom at the expense of the public interest. It is government more than at any time since the early 1900s in the grasp of business/industrial/financial interests.
- It is a movement that aids the rich in getting richer while doing little for the average American or the poor, showing profound disregard for them.
- It is a movement that, in the guise of protecting us from terrorists, infringes on our constitutional free-doms.
- It is a movement whose philosophy runs counter to America's historic values and our founding documents and is destructive of the American social contract.
- It is a movement out of step with mainstream America.

The choice is clear. We, as a people, can either be true to our liberal roots and stand tall or bend our collective knee to the new conservative taskmasters.

Democrats/Liberals are now and always have been strong on the economy, strong on the family, strong on social obligations, strong on social rights, and strong on defense. Democrats/Liberals have understood the inherent mix of liberal and conservative elements in the Declaration and the Bill of Rights and have seen how both are not only compatible but also essential to our form of government and the support of the people. That was especially true of President Clinton, much to the consternation of the Republicans/Conservatives.

Democrats/Liberals must build on their strong past and create a vision for the future. They must bring together the best and brightest minds in this country to develop a combina- tion of fresh government policies that not just respond to the changed assumptions of the world we live in but help shape or create new structures and assumptions that will take our country safely through this century.

- All Democrats/Liberals must denounce the policies of the Bush administration for what they are and rouse all moderates and liberals, regardless of party affiliation, to fight this ominous new Religious/Conservative movement.

- They must rally the country behind the American flag of liberty and justice for all, of the basic right of each and every person to have an equal opportunity to make the most of their lives. And, they must clearly explain the essential role of government under the American social contract, starting with the words of the Declaration of Independence, to help secure those rights for all Americans.

- They must fight to make the American dream a reality for an ever-expanding segment of the American public by improving educational, health, and employment opportunities for all Americans. To help accomplish that goal, they must reverse the trend of increasing income and wealth inequality through new government and private policies and programs that support the growth of a vigorous and diverse local economy and work force.

- They must work to make all Americans feel safer in their homes and on their streets, while remaining true to the fundamental rights guaranteed by our Constitution.

- They must argue for environmental, energy, and tax policies that are true to the American social contract and strike a fair balance between the property rights of individuals and business and the greater public good— policies that support the growth of business and the economy while protecting the long-term interests of the American public. The hold of business/industrial/financial interests on American governmental policy must be broken. Government must represent all the people.

- They must reengage that portion of the American public that has dropped out of our participatory democracy by speaking to their concerns, by reinvigorating the American social contract, and by showing them that there is a very real difference between Democrats and Republicans.

- They must craft a new foreign policy consistent with our American liberal roots that, together with revitalized domestic policies, will restore America's standing as the leading voice of freedom in the world.

By doing so, we will build a stronger, more secure America and enable all Americans to stand up proud, for themselves and for their country.

ACKNOWLEDGEMENTS

THIS BOOK WOULD not have been possible without the guidance, intelligence, and moral support of good friends, colleagues and family. Walter H. White, Jr., Marlan Buddingh, Michael Phillips, and Peter Hirsch each read an early draft of the work and provided me with a wealth of detailed comments and suggestions that greatly improved the book. Elaine Weiss, Isabelle Nicholson, Sonja Rein, and James Schmiechen provided me with valuable overall feedback on the book and its worth. Ken Carls and Malcolm McDonald provided me with very helpful technical advice regarding the book. Chris Griffin and William Haltom believed in me and my cause. Without the support of these wonderful people and others, it would have been difficult to persevere, complete the book, and obtain the pre-publication endorsements I have received. I also wish to thank Virtualbookworm.com Publisher Bobby Bernshausen without whom this book would not have seen the light of day nor reached its intended audience, as well as Don Ness for creating an effective design for the book's cover, which is so important in the book's successful marketing.

NOTES

[1] U.S. Bureau of the Census, *The Changing Shape of the Nation's Income Distribution, 1947–98.*

[2] U.S. Bureau of the Census, *Money Income in the United States: 2001,* Appendix A-2, Share of Aggregate Income Received by Each Fifth and Top 5% of Households, 1967-2001, September 2002.

[3] U.S. Federal Reserve Bank, *Recent Changes in U.S. Family Finances: Evidence from the 1998 and 2001 Survey of Consumer Finances,* Table 3, Family Net Worth by Selected Characteristics of Families, January 2003.

[4] Economic Policy Institute, *The State of Working America 2002–2003,* Press Release, 2002.

[5] ibid., Table 2.4 Hourly and Weekly Earnings of Private Production and Non-Supervisory Workers, 1947–2001.

[6] U.S. Bureau of the Census, *Poverty in the United States, 2001,* Table 1. Age, Sex, Household Relationship, Race and Hispanic Origin - Poverty Status of People by Selected Characteristics in 2001.

[7] ibid., Table 16a. Poverty Status of Families by Type of Family, Age of Householder, and Number of Children: 2001.

[8] U.S. Federal Election Commission, National Voter Turnout in Federal Elections: 1960–1996, and Voter Registration and Turnout 2000.

[9] The Gallup Organization, as reported in *Time,* January 19, 2004, p.21.

[10] The Harris Poll, No. 5, January 29, 2003.

[11] Ted Halstead, "The American Paradox," *The Atlantic,* January/February 2003, p.123–125.

[12] U.S. National Center for Education Statistics, "The Condition of Education, 1995," Public School District Funding Differences, September 1995.

[13] U.S. National Center for Education Statistics, "Current Expenditures per Student 1998-99," Summary.

[14] Children's Defense Fund, "Increase Investments in Head Start," August 19, 2003, http://www.childrensdefebse,org.

[15] ibid.

[16] U.S. Bureau of the Census, *Health Insurance Coverage: 2001,* Highlights, September 30, 2002,

[17] Carolynn Race, "Support Child Nutrition Programs," *The Washington Report,* March/April 2003, http://www.pcusa.org/washington/mar_apr03.htm.

[18] Shannon Brownlee, "The Overtreated American," *The Atlantic,* January/February 2003, p.89.

[19] Steffie Wolhandler, et al., "Proposal of the Physicians' Working Group for Single-Payer National Health Insurance," *JAMA.* 2003; 290:798–805.

[20] John M. Karon, PhD et al, "HIV in the United States at the Turn of the Century: An Epidemic in Transition," *American Journal of Public Health,* vol. 91(7), July 2001, pp 1060-106.

[21] Center for Disease Control and Prevention, *U.S. HIV and AIDS cases reported through December 2001, Year-end edition,* Vol.13, No.2, HIV/AIDS Surveillance Reports, Table 6: HIV infection cases by age group, exposure category, and sex, reported through December 2001; and Table 14: HIV infection cases in adolescents and adults under age 25, by sex and exposure category, reported through December 2001.

[22] U.S. Centers for Disease Control and Prevention, "Advancing HIV Prevention: New Strategies for a Changing Epidemic, United States 2003," MMWR, vol. 52, no.15, 320-332, April 18, 2003.

[23] Erica Goode, "Certain Words Can Trip Up AIDS Grants, Scientists Say," *The New York Times,* April 18, 2003, p.A10.

[24] Peggy Simpson, "AIDS Bill to Export 'Abstinence Only' to Africa," *WomensENews,* May, 27, 2003, http://www.womensenews.org/article.cfm/dyn/aid/1344/context/archive.

[25] Laura Meckler, "Carmona Playing Safe as Surgeon General," *Associated Press,* May 7, 2003.

[26] Susan A. Cohen, "Abortion Politics and U.S. Population Aid: Coping with a Complex New Law," *International Family Planning Perspectives,* vol. 26, no. 3, September 2000.

[27] The Harris Poll #27, June 13, 2001.

[28] The Harris Poll, New Witeck-Combs/Harris Interactive Research Shows Broad Public Support on Right to Privacy, Press Release, May 6, 2003.

[29] Human Rights Campaign Press Release, August 1, 2003.

[30] Human Rights Campaign, "Workplace Non-Discrimination Policies That Include Sexual Orientation," March 13, 2004, http://www.hrc.org/Template.cfm?Section=Non-Discrimination_Policies&Template=/TaggedPage/TaggedPageDisplay.cfm&TPLID=26&ContentID=13308h.

[31] *Lawrence v. Texas,* 539 U.S. _____ (2003).

[32] Patrick Buchanan, Speech to the Republican National Convention, August 17, 1992.

[33] "Episcopal Leaders Approve Gay Bishop," *ABC News Online,* August 6, 2003. http://www.abc.net.au/news/newsitems/s918253.htm.

[34] A Pastoral Letter, Concerned Clergy in West Michigan, October, 2001.

[35] Religious Coalition for the Freedom to Marry, Press Conference, June 5, 2003.

[36] ABC News/Washington Post Poll. Jan. 15–18, 2004.

[37] Cathy Lynn Grossman, "Gay 'Civil Union' Not as Divisive as 'Marriage'," *USA Today,* January 14, 2004, p, D6.

[38] E. Ferrero, J, Freker, and T. Foster, *Too High A Price: The Case Against Restricting Gay Parenting,* Summary, ACLU Lesbian & Gay Rights Project, 2003.

[39] John Conroy, "Deaf to the Screams," *The Reader,* August 1, 2003, vol. 32, no. 44, p.1.

[40] Eric Lichtblau, "Bush Seeks to Expand Access to Private Data and Forced Testimony," *The New York Times,* September 14, 2003, p.20.

[41] ibid.

[42] Natural Resources Defense Council, *Rewriting the Rules, Year-End Report 2002: The Bush Administration's Assault on the Environment,* Press Release, 2003.

[43] ibid.

[44] ibid.

[45] National Resources Defense Council, "DOE Attempting Legislative End-Run Around Court Ruling on Nuke Waste," July 17, 2003, http://www.nrdc.org/bushrecord/nuclear_disposal.asp#1377.

[46] "Bush's Air Pollution Plan Creates Stir," *CBS News,* July 30, 2002, http://www.cbsnews.com/stories/2002/06/13/politics/main512093.shtml.

[47] National Resources Defense Council, "Bush's Forest Proposal a 'Smokescreen,' says NRDC," August 22, 2002, http://www.nrdc.org/media/pressreleases/020822.asp.

[48] Environmental Protection Agency, *Final Report to Congress on Benefits and Costs of the Clean Air Act 1970–1990*, Summary of Results, EPA 410-R-97-002; and "New Report Shows Benefits of 1990 Clean Air Act Amendments Outweigh Costs by Four-to-One Margin," Press Release, November 16, 1999.

[49] "The Energy Crisis," *Time,* July 21, 2003, p.38.

[50] ibid.

[51] ibid. p. 39.

[52] Bayon, Ricardo, "The Fuel Subsidy We Need," *The Atlantic,* January/February 2003, p. 118.

[53] National Geographic, citing U.S. government statistics from 1998, www.nationalgeographic.com.

[54] U.S. Government Accounting Office, "The High-Speed Rail Investment Act of 2001," June 25, 2001.

[55] U.S. Bureau of the Census, *Historical Income Tables,* Table F-3. Mean Income Received by Each Fifth and Top 5 Percent of Families (All Races): 1966 to 2001.

[56] Nicholas Johnson, and Iris J. Law, "Are State Taxes Becoming More Regressive?" Summary, Center on Budget and Policy Priorities, October 1997.

[57] William Rivers Pitt, "The Mendacity Index," *Washington Monthly,* September 2003.

[58] U.S. Congressional Budget Office, *The Budget and Economic Outlook: Fiscal Years 2003–2012,* Table 1. Revenues, Outlays, Surpluses, Deficits, and Debt Held by the Public, 1962-2002, January 2002.

[59] U.S. Congressional Budget Office, *The Budget and Economic Outlook: Fiscal Years 2005–2014,* Summary, Table 1.1, January 2004.

[60] U.S. Bureau of Labor Statistics, Unemployment Rate, LNS14000000, Labor Force Statistics from the Current Population Survey.

[61] U.S. Bureau of Labor Statistics, Total Nonfarm Employment, CES0000000001, National Employment, Hours, and Earnings.

[62] Robert Kuttner, "War Distracts from Bush's Budget Cuts," *Boston Globe,* March 26, 2003.

[63] "Budget Plans Interfere with Promises of 'No Child Left Behind'," Leadership Conference on Civil Rights, March 18, 2003.

[64] U.S. Congressional Budget Office, *The Budget and Economic Outlook: An Update,* Summary, Table 1. Revenues, Outlays, Surpluses, Deficits, and Debt Held by the Public, 1962-2002, August 2003.

[65] David Friedman, "One-Dimensional Growth," *The Atlantic,* January/February 2003, p.110.

[66] ibid.

[67] Pete Engardio, Aaron Bernstein, and Manjeet Kripalani, "The New Global Job Shift," *Newsweek,* February 3, 2003.

[68] ibid.

[69] Porter, Eduardo, "The Bright Side of Sending Jobs Overseas", *The New York Times*, February 15, 2004, p. wk3

[70] Hernando De Soto, *The Mystery of Capital*, Basic Books, 2000.

[71] Michael Duffy, and Massimo Calabresi, "Letting Up on Osama," *Time*, August 11, 2003, p. 15.

[72] Environmental Working Group, USDA Farming Subsidies 2001, EWG Farm Subsidy Database, 2003.

[73] Barry Bearak, "Why People Still Starve," *The New York Times* Magazine, July 13, 2003, p.36.

[74] Environmental Working Group, U.S. Summary, EWG Farm Subsidy Database, 2003.

[75] Barry Bearak, op. cit.

[76] Nicholas Stern, "World Bank Chief Economist Urges Cuts in Rich Country Agricultural Subsidies," speech excerpts, November 19, 2002, http://web.worldbank.org/WBSITE/EXTERNAL/NEWS/0,,content MDK:20076448~menuPK:34463~pagePK:34370~piPK:34424~the SitePK:4607,00.html.